PENNINE
MOUNTAINS
The Cheviots, the Northern Moors, the Howgill Fells, the Yorkshire Dales and High Peak

Also by Terry Marsh

The Summits of Snowdonia
The Mountains of Wales
The Lake Mountains: One
The Lake Mountains: Two

British Library Cataloguing in Publication Data
Marsh, Terry
  The Pennine mountains: a walker's guide to
  the Cheviot Hills, the Northern Moors,
  the Howgill Fells, the Yorkshire Dales
  and the High Peak
  1. England. Pennines. Recreations.
  Walking—visitor's guide
  I. Title
  796.5'22'09428
  ISBN 0-340-43039-7

All photographs by the author

THE
PENNINE
MOUNTAINS

The Cheviots, the Northern Moors, the Howgill Fells, the Yorkshire Dales and High Peak

TERRY MARSH

Hodder & Stoughton

LONDON SYDNEY AUCKLAND TORONTO

Acknowledgements

Four books ago I set out in the naive belief that writing was a solitary occupation. In many respects that remains true, but as my travels have taken me throughout England and Wales so a team has developed to assist me in my task. Once again Allan Rimmer has cast his knowledgeable eye over the draft manuscript for me, eager, too, to check whether my research would deny his claim to have ascended every mountain in England and Wales. Tim Owen, in the Ordnance Survey at Southampton, double-checked all the heights and map references, while the library staff of the Department of Leisure in Wigan produced all manner of books and information. And in the same way the staff of the Ordnance Survey Record Map Library made all the necessary maps available to me, and the space in which to consult them, for which I am immensely grateful.

A special thanks goes to all those who accompanied me on this particular journey, especially Frances, and Albert, who fretted when rain threatened to cancel his weekend jaunts, and to Tom, whom we nearly lost in a bog on Kinder.

Contents

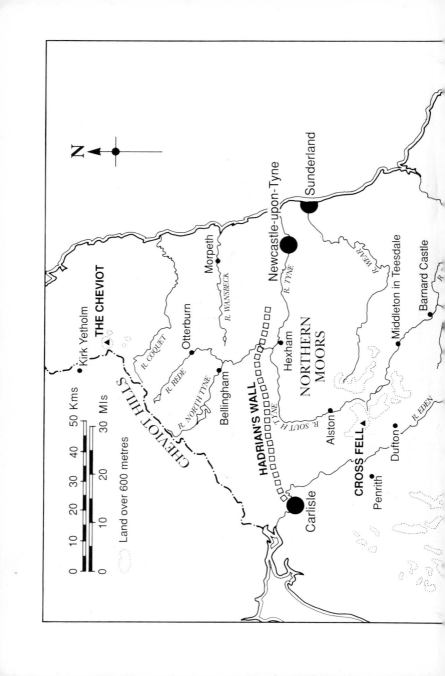

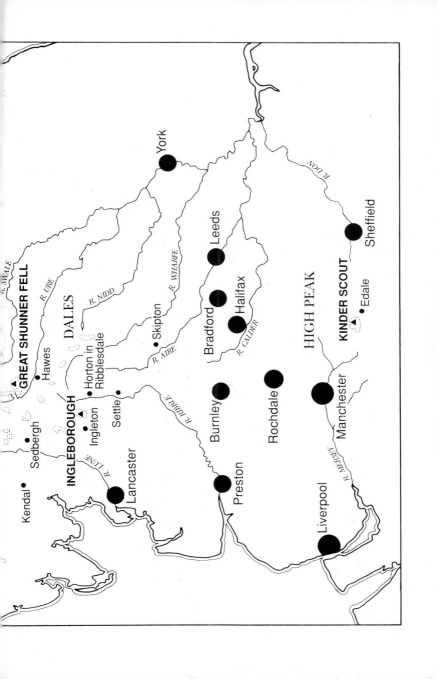

Introduction

Fresh from two years preparing *The Lake Mountains*, during which time I re-ascended almost every mountain in Lakeland, and that preceded by some four years working on *The Mountains of Wales* and *The Summits of Snowdonia*, I ventured into the Pennines not a little apprehensive. The Lake District possessed fine, detailed, craggy mountains compressed into a compact, easily accessible area; while the mountains of Wales, more spread out, equally craggy, just as accessible, stood as a proud challenge to all walkers and climbers. But the reputation of the Pennines had gone before them . . . bleak moorland summits, often shrouded in mist, riven by deep, slimy, black peat hags, and nowhere boasting even the slightest hint of grandeur. Camden wrote in the sixteenth century of "mountains waste, solitary, unpleasant and unsightly". Housman mentions "numerous and extensive bleak moors".

And I fell for it! After all, I'd dabbled on the Three Peaks of the Yorkshire Dales (not the best place to start), in passing made eyes at the Peak District for many years, and heard masses of what turned out to be horrendous gobbledegook about the Pennine Way. So, my conditioning underpinned by Wainwright, that redoubtable champion of every walker's cause, who twenty or so years ago completed his unique *Pennine Way Companion* with the words "Well, I'm glad it's finished, I must say", I ventured forth. With companions to hand, and maps and compass flapping briskly into action at the slightest sign of mist, I tramped many a long moorland mile only to discover, happily, that the Pennines more than hold their own, and provide splendid, beautiful and enjoyable alternatives to everything the Lake District and Wales have to offer.

The Pennines are unquestionably the backbone of Eng-

◄ *Nicol's Chair: High Cup Nick.*

land, albeit a rather disjointed backbone; to speak of them as a chain merely serves to draw attention to the weak links, the places where the central spinal mass has been eroded to leave behind quite distinct groups of hills and moors, separated by wide valleys and high moorland plains. Geographers would tell you that the Pennines are neither a chain nor a range of mountains, but simply a broad uplift, and that what many would regard as Pennine country means quite different things in different places.

To compound this identity crisis it is worth nothing that even the name 'Pennine' is of doubtful origin, a literary forgery, in fact. In 1747, a Professor of English in Copenhagen, Charles Bertram, claimed discovery of a fourteenth-century document describing Britain in Roman times. Britain, the document said, was divided by a chain of mountains called the Penine Alps (*Alpes Penina*). This led later geologists to adopt the name 'Penine', which subsequently acquired an additional 'n'. Bertram's document, however, turned out to be a forgery, though he may well have been inspired by Camden's definition of the Pennine Chain contained in *Britannia*: "It runs like as Apennine in Italy, through the middest of England, with a continued ridge, rising more with continued tops and cliffs one after another ever as far as Scotland. Here they are called 'Mooreland', after a while the Peak, Blackstone Edge, the Craven, the Stainmore and at length Cheviot." Everyone, it seems, shows a tendency to describe the Pennines in a south to north direction, betraying, perhaps, that many of the first explorers and chroniclers to the region came from the south; even the Pennine Way is considered to start in Edale rather than Kirk Yetholm, though some walkers prefer the comparative solitude of a north–south traverse. There is no logical argument to support this inversion, so in this book the Pennines are described from the top down.

The principal rocks of the Pennines belong to the Carboniferous Period, an era lasting some eighty million years, beginning about 350 million years ago, and have three main divisions – limestone, millstone grit and coal measures. These three divisions were later folded upwards, and exposed over millions of years to erosion by wind, water and ice. Most of the coal, and a lot of the gritstone, was swept from the tops of the hills, though enough gritstone remained in places to leave us today with the distinctive scenery of the Peak, for example. The remaining limestone itself was then attacked by water to form dales, caverns and gorges.

Other rocks do occur, remnants of earlier and later formations. Volcanic action took place both in Derbyshire and in the Cheviots, and there are the fine basaltic rocks of the Whin Sill, though these rocks intruded in the strata over an area stretching from the Farne Islands to Upper Teesdale, and are responsible for the falls of High Force and Cauldron Snout, the fine crags of High Cup Nick and the undulating heights followed by parts of Hadrian's Wall.

The geological structure of the Pennines is monoclinal, the rocks being for the most part abruptly cut off in the west by down-folding and faulting, and tilted gently towards the east. Once the limestone, millstone and coal measures of the Carboniferous Period had been laid down there began the greatest era of earth movements, during Permian times (207–230 million years ago). It was at this time, for example, that the great domed shapes of the Howgill Fells were formed and later isolated by a complicated process of faulting from the Askrigg massif, a great central block of unfolded rocks, along a fault known as the Dent Line. It is further south, in Craven, however, that the oldest rocks occur, at Chapel-le-Dale and Horton-in-Ribblesdale, where slates with bands of grit, known as Ingleton granite, are to be found.

The uplifting of the Permian times formed the massive, elongated ridge, which is the principal feature of the Pennines today. At one time it reached considerable height, only to be denuded and moulded by the agents of erosion to the softer, rounded form now familiar to everyone. But it is the variety given to the geology by local peculiarities which makes a study of the Pennines a fascinating pastime. In Upper Teesdale, for example, limestone has had its structure changed by baking in molten basalt. With the subsequent action of weathering this became the 'sugar' limestone favoured by alpine flora, and explains why the Nature Conservancy Council are at such pains to protect this spectacular heritage. At High Cup Nick and High Force molten material has cooled and hardened to form the Great Whin Sill, and given us some remarkable scenery. Other hot rocks from the earth's depths cooled to become galena (lead ore) and barytes, and provided man with a profitable living for many years.

Before man, however, from studies in numerous caves, we have a picture of a much younger Pennine world, tenanted by animals now associated with tropical Africa – elephant, hyena and lion, and in later, much colder conditions woolly rhinoceros, followed, during the tundral conditions after the last Ice Age, by animals normally found beyond the Arctic Circle – reindeer, Arctic fox and hare, elk and lynx.

In the millions of years unseen by man, conditions softened. The last ice withdrew from the high corrie basins, leaving their indelible scars to remain forever, to be camouflaged by a spread of lichens, Arctic and alpine plants, dwarf trees, notably willow, juniper and birch. In warmer wetter times trees spread higher on to the mountainsides, beyond which grew an immensely rich carpet of grasses, heaths and sedges.

About 8000 years ago, man appeared in the Pennines, hunting parties summering on the hillsides and fishing in the glacial lakes, and following the valley sides beneath the edges of gritstone. Later, the Celts came, naming rivers like the Wharfe and the Nidd; Angles and Danes populated the valleys, while the Norse peopled the higher ground. All three left a legacy of place-names that lives on today: Anglian place-names are frequently suffixed by *ley* (a clearing) and *tun* (a farmstead, usually surrounded by a wall), while Danish names end in *by* and *thorp*. The Norsemen provided us with the names *fell*, *beck*, *moss*, *heath* and *gill*.

These people and their descendants ravaged the countryside, denuding the landscape of its trees here as they had done elsewhere, and imposed boundary lines where none had existed or were needed. When dry-stone walls were built, boundaries produced a state of the art patchwork, and sometimes idiotic regularity, fuelled by the dictates of the Enclosure Commissioners whose desk-decreed straight lines were frequently translated into ludicrous results. But whatever may have been done to it, there is no escaping the fact that it is the uniqueness of this much maligned landscape that man now seeks for his pleasure. A motorised traveller gains a broad sense of geological change as he journeys through the Pennines, but it is the walker who achieves a deeper understanding, not least because of the way the changes of geological structure affect his progress, as on Ingleborough, for example, where in one trek you can pass from limestone to gritstone, or at either end of the Pennines, among the Cheviot Hills or around Kinder and Bleaklow, where the transition from springy turf to leg-wearying bog is most pronounced.

Many parts of the Pennines have a well-established history of tourism. During the seventeenth century many travellers came to view the wonders of the Peak, while the nineteenth-century spread of the railways opened up the countryside to anyone who could afford the fare. But for many years great tracts of the Pennines were the play-ground of the privileged few. Streams were private and patrolled by water bailiffs, while the moors were the strict preserve of the grouse-shooting fraternity. The ordinary mortal was most adamantly and often energetically barred from the hills. This state of affairs, thankfully, did not last, and in 1932 hundreds of people indulged in a mass trespass on Kinder Scout in defiance of the gamekeepers. Though by no means the first mass trespass (walkers in and around Bolton effected a mass trespass on Winter Hill in 1896), it led to the Access to Mountains Act which formalised access rights for walkers but, alas, in a vague and insubstantial way so far as the Pennines were concerned. It was only during the postwar years, with the establishment of national parks, under the National Parks and Access to the Countryside Act, 1949, that access vastly improved.

Though by no means the norm there are still large areas, notably in the Northern Pennines (ironically an area recently designated an Area of Outstanding Natural Beauty), where access other than along established rights of way is jealously guarded. During the grouse-shooting season (August–October) it is wise to stay off known grouse moors without permission; for the rest of the year, especially in the breeding season, be sensitive to the effects of your intrusion on these wild and beautiful moors. Faced with the letter of the law each walker must examine his or her own conscience; I have never been turned off open moorland, though I know people who have. It's a dilemma we all have to face. Not all walking needs to be summit-orientated, there are many legitimate valley walks that should incur the wrath of no one – up Hilton Gill and down High Cup Gill, for example. But if you want to conquer Mickle Fell you need to step across the threshold and on to private land. One thing is certain, however, so far as access is concerned: inconsiderate behaviour, damage to property, and litter are sure ways of inciting opposition.

Nor was it only the private landowners who sought to keep people off their land. For many years the Forestry Commission did likewise, as, too, did the water authorities. Thankfully, these policies of exclusion have now been almost totally reversed, the area around Kielder in the Cheviots being perhaps the best example of what can be achieved where these opposing demands reach a compromise.

The Pennine Way, too, was an access landmark and a fine achievement, though it did not come into being until

24th April 1965. The idea was inspired by the Appalachian Trail in America, and first put forward by the late Tom Stephenson in an article in the *Daily Herald* in 1935. It is today a much-loved and much-hated concoction of natural lines and wayward wandering that takes you through the wealth and variety of scenery so typical of this remarkable region. In their second annual report the National Parks Commission, who had been charged with the responsibility of submitting proposals for the creation of long-distance routes, said: "The Pennine Way will be a strenuous high-level route through predominantly wild country and is intended for walkers of some experience. It will involve a fair element of physical exertion and a willingness to endure rough going."

This last comment sums up the Pennines. But they are far from the totally boggy, unremitting, windswept upland desert some might have you believe. They are not desolate and forlorn, but infinitely varied, rich in flora and fauna, abundant in

> Long-legged walks in lowering clouds
> On peaty plateaux far from crowds.

I came to the Pennine Mountains tinged with reservation; now I can commend them without any.

Explanatory Notes

None of the routes described presents technical problems in good weather conditions in summer, and the majority may also be completed in good winter conditions. Many routes, however, lie across bleak and often featureless moorland mountains where mist becomes a major hazard. Throughout the book I have assumed that readers are competent navigators, skilled in map and compass technique, and know how to clothe and protect themselves effectively. In winter, with snow and ice on the ground, an ice-axe is always essential, as is the knowledge to use it properly, and there will be times and places when crampons greatly facilitate progress. It is foolhardy to think of venturing into the mountainous terrain of the Pennines without experience in these fundamental skills.

Table 1 – set out on pages 19–22 – lists, in order of altitude, all elevations of 600 metres or more throughout the length and breadth of the Pennines with a minimum of 30 metres of re-ascent from all directions, including summits of sufficient topographical merit with less re-ascent. It also contains an appendix of all other named summits over 600 metres with less than 30 metres of re-ascent, though I have not included elevations which have no measurable re-ascent. The lists are based on a survey conducted in April, 1987 of the latest 1:10 000 scale Ordnance Survey maps.

Maps In the preparation of Table 1 I have used 1:10 000 maps in order to pinpoint exactly where the highest point on any summit lies – it isn't always the trig point! – and so that I can carefully measure the amount of re-ascent. Map references are to the nearest 100 metres when converted for use on 1:50 000 maps.

The Pennines have the advantage, however, of being in part covered on a number of the excellent Outdoor Leisure Maps produced by the Ordnance Survey, which are to a scale of 1:25 000 (2½ inches to a mile). In the main these concentrate on the High Peak and the Yorkshire Dales, and readers will benefit considerably from using these more detailed maps on which many of the features I have mentioned as being "not named on the 1:50 000 map" are clearly identified.

Heights Heights are the latest available from the Ordnance Survey and may occasionally differ from those on published maps. There are also a few instances where a summit has a number of points of the same height, some distance apart. Where this occurs I have supplied additional map references.

If there is no height available, the height shown in the Tables is that of the highest contour ring. In these cases the height is followed by the letter c.

Distances and Ascent These are approximate and have been rounded up or down, but they are sufficiently accurate to allow you to calculate times using Naismith's or other rules.

Paths There are numerous paths throughout the Pennines, far more than I have detailed in this book. It should be noted however that *any reference to paths or other lines of ascent does not imply that a right of way exists.*

Names The Ordnance Survey spelling has been used throughout, taken from the 1:10 000 maps, and I have included alternative names generally in use (in parentheses). If there is no name on any map, then the name commonly accepted either locally or among hill-walkers has been used. In the absence of anything, a rare occurrence, the expression 'Unnamed summit' has been adopted, next to which, for identification purposes, has been given the name of the nearest named summit or prominent feature.

Section and Section Names are quite arbitrary, and centre on one or more principal hills or other geographical features. No one should take them too seriously, they are essentially creatures of convenience which came about after much fruitless endeavour to impose a 'tidy' framework on an unframeable terrain.

Each section begins with a separate table of all the heights contained within that section, and includes all the 600-metre summits plus many lesser heights which have significant re-ascent and/or which stand sufficiently distant from higher mountains to be worthy of our attention in their own right.

Access I have walked without challenge throughout the Pennines for many years, and most walkers will enjoy the same freedom, especially if they stick to orthodox lines of ascent. The exploration of the hills is something to be enjoyed by everyone, and wandering freely across trackless ground is part of that pleasure. This general freedom, achieved and maintained only by considerate walkers, should not be interpreted as a licence to clamber over walls and fences indiscriminately causing damage, or to tramp through fields of crops. And to travel anywhere on the hills with a dog that is not held on a leash is inviting the wrath, rightly so, of the men and women who earn a living from 'the Backbone of England'.

Photography All the photographs in this book are my own, taken exclusively on a now much-battered Olympus OM-1n primarily with a Zuiko 35mm f2.8 lens, though a Tamron 28mm–80mm zoom was occasionally used. A yellow-green filter (Hoya G(XO)) always occupied the front of the lenses other than in extremely poor light. The film was Agfapan 100 Professional (rated at normal speed), developed in Rodinal. The subsequent prints were on Kentmere Grade 3 glossy paper developed in Agfa Neutol (normal dilution).

Colour photographs were, of course, taken at the same time, using Agfachrome 100 RS Professional, trade processed. An Olympus OM-4n with the Tamron lens, sporting a Hoya multi-coated UV(O) filter, always proved reliable.

Table 1

The 600-metre mountains of the Pennines arranged in order of altitude with a minimum of 30 metres of re-ascent from all directions, including summits of sufficient topographical merit with less re-ascent.

	HEIGHT (m)		MAP REF.	SECTION NUMBER	SECTION NAME
1	893	Cross Fell	687343	2	Northern Moors
2	848	Great Dun Fell	710322	2	Northern Moors
3	842	Little Dun Fell	704330	2	Northern Moors
4	815	The Cheviot	909205	1	Cheviot Hills
5	794	Knock Fell (Green Fell)	722303	2	Northern Moors
6	788	Mickle Fell	804243	2	Northern Moors
7	767	Meldon Hill	772291	2	Northern Moors
8	748	Burton Fell (Little Fell) (Hilton Fell)	781223	2	Northern Moors
9	746	Burnhope Seat	788375	2	Northern Moors
10	736	Whernside	739816	4	Dales
11	723	Ingleborough	741746	4	Dales
12	716	Great Shunner Fell	849973	4	Dales
13	714	Hedgehope Hill	944198	1	Cheviot Hills
14	710c	Dead Stones	794399	2	Northern Moors
15	709	High Seat (Mallerstang Edge)	802012	4	Dales
16	709	Melmerby Fell	652380	2	Northern Moors
17	708	Wild Boar Fell	758988 760988 761985	4	Dales
18	708	Great Stony Hill	824359	2	Northern Moors
19	704	Great Whernside	002739	4	Dales
20	703	Chapelfell Top (Langdon Fell)	876346	2	Northern Moors
21	702	Buckden Pike	961788	4	Dales
22	698	Unnamed summit (Backstone Edge)	726277	2	Northern Moors
23	694	Pen y Ghent	838734	4	Dales
24	689	Hugh Seat	809991	4	Dales
25	687	Great Coum	701836	4	Dales
26	686	Round Hill	744361	2	Northern Moors
27	681	Swarth Fell	756967	4	Dales
28	680c	Plover Hill	849752	4	Dales
29	678	Baugh Fell (Tarn Rigg Hill)	741916	4	Dales
30	676	The Calf	667971	3	Howgills
31	676	Baugh Fell (Knoutberry Haw)	731919	4	Dales
32	675	Lovely Seat	879951	4	Dales
33	675	Murton Fell	754246	2	Northern Moors

34	675	Outberry Plain	923326	2	Northern Moors
35	674	Calders (Brant Fell)	671960	3	Howgills
36	673	Killhope Law	819448	2	Northern Moors
37	672	Great Knoutberry Hill (Widdale Fell)	789872	4	Dales
38	672	Rogan's Seat	919031	4	Dales
39	672	Bram Rigg Top	668965	3	Howgills
40	668	Dodd Fell Hill	841846	4	Dales
41	668	Fountains Fell (North Summit)	864716	4	Dales
42	668	Unnamed summit (Water Crag)	929046	4	Dales
43	667	Lunds Fell	809971	4	Dales
44	664	Black Fell	648444	2	Northern Moors
45	662	Nine Standards Rigg	825061	4	Dales
46	662	Fountains Fell (South Summit)	869708	4	Dales
47	656	Grey Nag	665476	2	Northern Moors
48	652	Comb Fell	924187	1	Cheviot Hills
49	651	Three Pikes	834343	2	Northern Moors
50	650	Simon Fell	755752	4	Dales
51	649	Herdship Fell	789332	2	Northern Moors
52	643	Yockenthwaite Moor	909811	4	Dales
53	640	Fell Head	649982	3	Howgills
54	639	Yarlside	686985	3	Howgills
55	636	Kinder Scout	084876 085875 087876	5	High Peak
56	634	Fiend's Fell	643406	2	Northern Moors
57	633	Bleaklow Head	092959	5	High Peak
58	627	Gragareth	688793	4	Dales
59	625	Randygill Top	687001	3	Howgills
60	624	Darnbrook Fell	884728	4	Dales
61	621	Cold Fell	606556	2	Northern Moors
62	620c	Tynehead Fell (Bellbeaver Rigg)	763350	2	Northern Moors
63	619	Windy Gyle	855152	1	Cheviot Hills
64	619	Bink Moss	875243	2	Northern Moors
65	615	Cushat Law	928137	1	Cheviot Hills
66	614	Drumaldrace (Wether Fell)	874867	4	Dales
67	614	Flinty Fell	771420 771422	2	Northern Moors
68	614	The Dodd	791458	2	Northern Moors
69	612	Burtree Fell	862432	2	Northern Moors
70	610	Bloodybush Edge	902143	1	Cheviot Hills
71	609	Thack Moor (Renwick Fell)	611463	2	Northern Moors
72	609	Calf Top	664856	4	Dales
73	609	Sugar Loaf	894768	4	Dales
74	608	Birks Fell	916764	4	Dales

75	605	The Schil	869223	1	Cheviot Hills
76	605	Arant Haw	662946	3	Howgills
77	605	Green Bell	699011	3	Howgills
78	604	Little Whernside	028776	4	Dales
79	604	Black Hill	873411	2	Northern Moors
80	602	Watch Hill (Graystone Edge)	628460	2	Northern Moors
81	602	High Green Field Knott (Cosh Knott)	845784	4	Dales
82	602	Peel Fell	{ 625997 626997 }	1	Cheviot Hills

Appendix to Table 1

Other named summits of over 600 metres, with less than 30 metres of re-ascent.

	MAP REF.	HEIGHT (m)	SECTION NUMBER	SECTION NAME	1:50 000 OS MAP
Cairn Hill	903195	777	1	Cheviot Hills	80
Auchope Cairn	891198	726	1	Cheviot Hills	80
Scaud Hill	795363	718	2	Northern Moors	91
Fendrith Hill	877333	696	2	Northern Moors	91/92
Arnside Rake*	786232	693	2	Northern Moors	91
Cronkley Fell (Long Crag)	843252	686	2	Northern Moors	91
Knapside Hill	646384	685	2	Northern Moors	91
Crag Hill	692833	682	4	Dales	98
Stony Rigg	664369	681	2	Northern Moors	91
Nag's Head	793409	678	2	Northern Moors	86/87
Brown Hill	662358	676	2	Northern Moors	91
Knoutberry Hill	803421	668	2	Northern Moors	86/87
Great Dummacks	679963	663	3	Howgills	98
Dora's Seat	888332	661	2	Northern Moors	91/92
White Mossy Hill*	829053	659	4	Dales	91/92
Little Shunner Fell*	859971	653	4	Dales	98
Swarth Fell Pike	761958	651	4	Dales	98
White Fell Head	661974	646	3	Howgills	97/98
Westernhope Moor	906334	645	2	Northern Moors	91/92
Viewing Hill	787338	640c	2	Northern Moors	91
Knoutberry Currack	{ 828981 829978 }	638	4	Dales	98
Tom Smith's Stone	655467	637	2	Northern Moors	86
Westend Moor	841437	634	2	Northern Moors	86/87
Noon Hill	854358	632	2	Northern Moors	91/92
Crowden Head	096881	632	5	High Peak	110
Bleaklow Hill	104964	630	5	High Peak	110
Green Hill	702820	628	4	Dales	98
Tor Mere Top	969765	628	4	Dales	98
Pikeman Hill	723382	625	2	Northern Moors	91
Hartside Height	651426	624	2	Northern Moors	86
Bush Howe	659981	623	3	Howgills	97/98
Warcop Fell	782201	622	2	Northern Moors	91

Shelf Moor (Higher Shelf Stones)	089948	621	5	High Peak	110
Long Fell	768200	620c	2	Northern Moors	91
Bullman Hills	705371	614	2	Northern Moors	91
Snowhope Hill	943344	610c	2	Northern Moors	91/92
Benty Hill	669431	609	2	Northern Moors	86
Carrs Hill (Racketgill Head★)	947311	608	2	Northern Moors	91/92
Nunnery Hill	769428	608	2	Northern Moors	86/87
Slack's Rigg	771363	607	2	Northern Moors	91
Firth Fell	926748	607	4	Dales	98
Horse Head	887780	605	4	Dales	98
Hartshorn★	115877	604	5	High Peak	110
Moss Top	906762	603	4	Dales	98
Grindslow Knoll	110868	601	5	High Peak	110
Brownber Head	845068	600c	2	Northern Moors	91/92

★ Denotes that the summit is not named on the 1:50 000 map

Section 1 – The Cheviot Hills

	MAP REFERENCE	HEIGHT (m)	1:50 000 OS MAP
The Cheviots			
The Cheviot	909205	815	74
Cairn Hill	903195	777	80
Auchope Cairn	891198	726	80
Hedgehope Hill	944198	714	74/80
Comb Fell	924187	652	80
Windy Gyle	855152	619	80
Cushat Law	928137	615	80
Bloodybush Edge	902143	610	80
The Schil	869223	605	74
The Curr	851233	564	74
Beefstand Hill	821144	561	80
Mozie Law	829150	552	80
Black Hag	862237	549	74
Lamb Hill	811133	511	80
Kielder			
Peel Fell	{ 626997 625997 }	602	80
Deadwater Fell	626972	569	80
Mid Fell	636984	561	80
Carlin Tooth	631024	551	80
Hartshorn Pike	628017	545	80

ROUTES

1.1   The Cheviot
1.2   Hedgehope Hill and Comb Fell
1.3   Auchope Cairn
1.4   The Schil
1.5   Windy Gyle
1.6   Bloodybush Edge
1.7   Cushat Law
1.8   Mozie Law, Beefstand Hill and Lamb Hill
1.9   Peel Fell from Kielder
1.10 Carter Fell from Carter Bar

Forming along their north-western flank the border between England and Scotland, the Cheviot Hills contain
some of the finest, if not *the* finest, walking country in the
whole of the Pennines. Unlike the rolling South Tyne
flatlands further south, they possess a shapely counten-
ance that is easy on the eye and which bears an invigorating
sense of distance and freedom. At the southern end the
lower hills around Kielder are swathed in forests where
roe deer flit among ranks of spruce like shadows in spring.
While to the north hilltop after hilltop undulates ever
higher to the broad flat mound that is The Cheviot itself.
In *Walking the Scottish Border* Bob Langley refers to these
benign giants as: "Good country, wild country, but with a
subtle gentleness that makes it seem like home."

The hills are a relatively recent range formed during the
Ice Age, with a mixture of volcanic rocks, glacial deposits
and granite, and for the most part comprise uncluttered
grassy slopes devoid of human habitation, except the
occasional hill farm or shepherd's hut. But it is a region
that has seldom known peace. The hills were inhabited
long ago by Neolithic man and the Beaker people, by the
Romans, who built such outposts as the Chew Green
camps, then by the Norse invaders. From the tenth
century they were the battlegrounds of the long war of
attrition between the Scots and the English, mostly made
up of reiving forays when a quick advantage could be
taken and long-standing feuds could be nurtured and
celebrated in border ballads. Occasionally the hills were
the crossroads for a military show of strength by the rival
monarchs. Now the battles here are the war games of
military training, for a good chunk of the central Cheviots
is an artillery range.

The Cheviots also comprise the highest ground in the
Northumberland National Park, Britain's most northerly
national park, one with few orthodox beauty spots or
craggy mountainsides, where virtue lies instead in the
subtle variety of form and colour among the hills and
valleys, and in its richness of flora and fauna. Excluded

from the national park is the vast area of Kielder Forest, reputedly the largest man-made forest in Europe. There are few major hills for walkers among the Kielder Forests, though many smaller ones (too numerous for the compass of this book) are well worth the effort of exploration. But both the forests and the accompanying reservoir are outstandingly beautiful and well managed. The forests have established themselves impressively within the space of just two generations, while work on the reservoir, part of the Kielder Water Scheme, only started in April 1976. The reservoir was filled by the spring of 1982. To avoid unsightly mud flats a second reservoir, Bakethin, was constructed at the upper end of Kielder Water, near the village, and this, together with the surrounding forest area, is a nature conservation area.

The fascinating thing about the Cheviot Hills is that they offer virtually limitless scope for the walker at all levels. Short circular walks, forest trails, lofty assaults on high mountain summits, and ultra-long excursions are all to be found here. The keys to this profusion are the long central border ridge (from Kielder to the Bowmont valley) and the many accompanying side valleys. A diligent walker may find enough nooks and crannies here to last a lifetime.

The geology is a complex study in itself, its invasion by mankind often of bloody, morbid, but continuing interest. While the flora and fauna is unbelievably rich in its diversity, from the exquisite Alpine varieties of Teesdale to the breathtaking carpets of wild and mountain pansies, bog asphodel and myrtle of the rolling Cheviots; and from moorland birds such as curlew, snipe, golden plover, sandpiper or grouse, to fleeting finches, pipits and hawks in the valleys.

Route 1.1 The Cheviot The Cheviot (909205) is the highest summit in the range of hills to which it lends its name. Far from boasting a fine monarchical topknot of rock, however, its summit is a vast peat bog; rainwater, unable to sink into the underlying granite, prevents the proper decomposition of heather, moss and grasses, forming, as a result, a ubiquitous black peat. It is the preponderance of peat which has earned The Cheviot an unfortunate reputation, but there is far worse and far more on Kinder and Bleaklow, which summits do not have The Cheviot's abundance of attractive valleys as surrounding compensation.

In 1728 Daniel Defoe ascended The Cheviot, expecting to encounter a knife-edged ridge, but was doubtless disappointed (or relieved) by what he found. By timing your visit to coincide with a prolonged dry spell you will evade the worst clutches of the bog, and make of The Cheviot an excursion comparable with any in the Pennines.

Numerous approaches suggest themselves – from Cocklawfoot or Uswayford, for example, or along the Pennine Way, which between Redesdale and the Bowmont valley sticks more or less to the border. But the finest begin in College valley to the north-west or Harthope valley to the north-east, both exquisitely delightful lines of approach.

1.1a From College valley College valley is a private valley to which consent for vehicle access is required. It is open to approximately 12 motor vehicles on any day except between the middle of April and the end of May when lambing is taking place. Permits may be obtained from Messrs. Sale and Partners, 18–20 Glendale Road, Wooler, Northumberland, NE71 6DW, who explain that the restriction on numbers is to keep the valley unspoiled, and because there are still a great number of people who enjoy walking in a traffic-free environment.

It is possible to drive along the valley as far as Mounthooly, but for a satisfying circuit, leave vehicles near the hall at 888252, and proceed along the roadway from there. In springtime and early summer the valley is delightful, with a wide variety of wild flowers and birds. Beyond Mounthooly a track continues uneventfully alongside College Burn, deteriorating finally to a narrow path leading directly into Hen Hole, a massive and impressive corrie and gorge fashioned from the rocks during the Ice Age, and down which College Burn cascades in a fine series of waterfalls. There are numerous tales and legends about Hen Hole; fairies once lived in the dank and mossy clefts by the falls; huntsmen were lured to their deaths by strange music, and Black Adam of Cheviot, a notorious freebooter, had his lair there. On one occasion he invaded a wedding party at Wooperton, robbed the guests and stabbed the bride. In a slightly different version he is said to have ravished the bride; either way the bridegroom was none too happy, and pursued him back to Hen Hole where, in attempting to jump the gorge, both men fell to their deaths.

There is a scrambly route through Hen Hole to the summit of The Cheviot, but this faces you with a larger share of bog than is necessary when an alternative, if longer, route is available. Follow instead the line of the footpath shown on the 1:50 000 map which runs on south then east and makes for a gash on the hillside known as Red Cribs (not named on the 1:50 000 map). The name surely comes from the colour of the soil, and was mentioned as long ago as 1597 as "Gribbheade, a passage and hyeway for the theefe." – there are still signs of an old drove road, obviously linking the valleys on either side of the border.

Before the Union of the Crowns in 1603, the border was divided into the East, Middle and West Marches, each under the charge of a warden whose luckless task it was to keep order in his area. A Memorandum of 1579 suggests that the decay of the English Marches was due to raids by the Scots, neglect of horses and arms, castles and forts being in unworthy hands, and deadly private feuds between many of the families, made worse by intermarrying.

A number of indistinct paths brings you finally to the Scottish border fence which should be followed first to Auchope Cairn, and then on to the fence junction (896194) at which the border makes a sharp dog-leg west. Here a less prominent fence runs initially eastwards and then north-eastwards to pass close to the trig, built on a high plinth, marking the summit of The Cheviot.

DISTANCE: 9.3 kilometres (5.8 miles)
ASCENT: 625 metres (2050 feet)

To return to the starting point the finest line is to descend along the fence, north-east, to the col between Lambden Burn and Hawsen Burn, and to turn west there, making for Goldscleugh to join a good track for the final stretch to the hall. There is a good path alongside the fence descending from the summit to the col, and only in the upper section of Lambden Burn is the path a little difficult to locate. This is principally because neither path from Lambden Burn or Hawsen Burn actually strikes the col, meeting instead a short way up the southern slopes of Broadhope Hill, at a gate. Walkers running short of time may feel tempted to descend rather more directly to Lambden Burn from the summit, but the going is both steep and arduous, and though lined with the threads of intermittent footpaths is not significantly quicker than continuing to the col.

It follows, of course, that the whole circuit may easily be reversed, with equal satisfaction, though the pull to The Cheviot from the col at the head of Lambden Burn is rather more noticeable than the gentler approach via Auchope Cairn and Cairn Hill.

1.1b From Harthope valley The Harthope valley, approached from Wooler, is a charming compliment to its neighbour further west, and equally attractive. The ascent of The Cheviot from this direction has much to commend it.

There is room to park near Hawsen Burn, and doing so facilitates an elongated circuit making the most of the valley and pursuing a safe (ie fence-accompanied) line across the boggy summit. Directions could not be simpler: follow the valley to its head on a wild col between Cairn

Hill and Comb Fell, and ascend north-west and then north to the top of Cairn Hill (marked by, yes, a large cairn), crossed by a fenceline. Follow the fence to the summit of The Cheviot.

DISTANCE: 8 kilometres (5 miles)
ASCENT: 575 metres (1885 feet)

Return by descending as described above to the col between Lambden Burn and Hawsen Burn, this time turning east to follow the bracken-clad banks of Hawsen Burn back to Harthope valley. As on the opposite side of the col, the initial whereabouts of footpaths shown on the map is often obscured by heather and bracken.

DISTANCE: 5.8 kilometres (3.6 miles)

Route 1.2 Hedgehope Hill and Comb Fell Viewed from the south, from Cushat Law, Comb Fell (924187) appears as a dull mound against the higher dull mound of The Cheviot: Hedgehope Hill (944198), on the other hand, has a fine profile, and is an attractive hill. Combining these two with The Cheviot is unquestionably one of the finest circuits in the Cheviots, and is highly recommended; the second half of this round, from the col between Comb Fell and Cairn Hill, being detailed in Route 1.1b.

It is a most delightful walk along Harthope Burn and Harthope Linn, but this leads you to Comb Fell first. Better is to tackle the steepness of Hedgehope Hill early in the day, and then, if not continuing the circuit to The Cheviot, dally down Harthope Linn where little effort is required.

There is room to park cars where Hawsen Burn enters the Harthope valley (953225), and the walk starts from here. Cross the road and follow a signposted path ('Hedgehope Hill') leading to the wooded shade of Harthope Burn, crossed by a wooden bridge. Beyond the burn ascend steadily on a clear path to make for the prominent knoll of Housey Crags. Nearly 400 million years ago this region was the scene of intense volcanic activity, starting with outbursts of immense explosive ferocity, followed by numerous lava flows. Later a dome of magma (molten rock) formed beneath the volcanoes of the Cheviot hills, and cooled to form granite. Where these two rock masses, the magma and the lava, met the intensity of the heat produced a harder ring of rock, a Metamorphic Aureole (now known locally and simply as 'Cheviot') of which Housey Crags and the adjacent Langlee Crags are formed. Much of this rock was eroded away by the action of ice during later glacial periods, but, as here, the occasional rock tor still stands above the surrounding terrain, aligned north to south to accord with the direction of the ice flow.

Pass behind Housey Crags and continue across a short damp stretch to Long Crags beyond which a path extends towards Hedgehope Hill. This path, however, is of little assistance in gaining the summit of Hedgehope Hill, and a better approach is to follow the line of the fence you encounter just after Long Crags, south to the boundary with the forestry plantation shown on the map. You should then pursue the boundary fence upwards, steeply in places, to the summit of Hedgehope Hill, the highest point of which is marked by a large cairn and trig. The view is quite remarkable.

DISTANCE: 3.7 kilometres (2.3 miles)
ASCENT: 475 metres (1560 feet)

The continuation to Comb Fell simply follows the fence-line and presents no difficulty, in spite of a short stretch of boggy ground. The summit, unmarked, lies on the first bump you reach.

DISTANCE: 2.3 kilometres (1.4 miles)
ASCENT: 85 metres (280 feet)

To return now to the head of the Harthope valley, or to continue the circuit to Cairn Hill, it is easiest to stay with the fenceline until it makes a prominent change of direction (south), and from that point trek across broken, boggy ground, rich in heather, to the col at the head of the valley from where your journey may be continued either by tackling the flanks of Cairn Hill or diving into the sheltered seclusion of Harthope. The return from Comb Fell to the col and along Harthope Linn, favoured by trout and the darting flight of wagtails and dippers, will extend your walk by a further 7.5 kilometres (4.7 miles).

The complete circuit of Hedgehope Hill, Comb Fell, Cairn Hill and The Cheviot, returning to the starting point as described in Route 1.1b, covers 15.5 kilometres (9.7 miles), with 790 metres (2590 feet) of ascent, and may rightfully be regarded as a classic walk.

Route 1.3 Auchope Cairn Auchope Cairn (891198) is little more than a satellite of The Cheviot, though sufficiently distant to merit attention in its own right. Much in its favour is its firmer going when conditions on the higher summit leave a good deal to be desired. The highest point is marked by a couple of large cairns with attractive views down the College valley, along the final section of the Pennine Way over The Schil, or towards the massive dome of The Cheviot itself. Many satisfying approaches may be made, especially from the side valleys branching from the main Bowmont valley, notably via Curr Burn, from Attonburn, and Cocklawfoot, for there are as many

The Schil (left) and The Cheviot.

permutations of approach as there was traffic across these border hills. The only difference is that today the walkers' purposes are for pleasure and exercise, not reiving and feuding.

The most satisfying ascent approaches by College valley and this route may be extended to include The Schil. Route 1.1a describes the approach and how to get a vehicle permit for access to the valley. By retracing one's steps from the summit, and pursuing the Pennine Way to The Schil and beyond, it is possible to gain a footpath descending eastwards, into England, and down alongside the woodland boundary containing Fleehope Burn. From the hall at 888252 the journey to Auchope Cairn, with the return over The Schil, will extend to 16 kilometres (10 miles), with 690 metres (2265 feet) of ascent.

Route 1.4 The Schil The Schil (869223) lies north-west of The Cheviot, and though easily overshadowed by the sheer bulk of the higher mountain still manages to capture the eye with its fine domelike shape and pointed summit. For Pennine Wayfarers travelling north, and coming so soon after the obligatory but tiring diversion to The Cheviot, it will no doubt inspire volumes of invective which, to be fair, it doesn't deserve. Perched neatly on the

Looking across the border moors to The Schil.

border between Scotland and England, its summit crown of rocks some 30 metres or so in the former, The Schil offers an excellent walk from both the Bowmont and College valleys, and is ample fare for one day.

1.4a From the College valley Route 1.1a describes the College valley approach (starting from the hall at 888252), and the means by which walkers wishing to enter this private valley may obtain permission to do so. Simply follow this delightful valley until the Hen Hole appears ahead, and then (or sooner) divert, right, to gain the border ridge. Follow the ridge fence northwards over a minor top, Birnie Brae, and on to The Schil.
DISTANCE: 7.5 kilometres (4.7 miles)
ASCENT: 430 metres (1410 feet)

1.4b From the Bowmont valley The more conventional route from the Bowmont valley is by the Pennine Way from Kirk Yetholm, though enterprising walkers and seekers of solitude will find an equally pleasant approach from Primsidemill and along Curr Burn. This is clearly marked on the 1:50 000 map, and needs little description; it brings one eventually to the col between The Curr and Black Hag where the Pennine Way is joined to pursue the border for the short remaining distance to the summit.
DISTANCE: 7.8 kilometres (4.9 miles)
ASCENT: 485 metres (1590 feet)

The standard route from the Bowmont valley tackles the Pennine Way, and is no less attractive for all the attention it receives. As is typical throughout much of the length of the Pennine Way it essentially caters for walkers travelling south to north, leaving many fundamental questions over the correct route unsignposted. The departure from Kirk Yetholm is a blatant example. Students of the Pennine Way will realise that the Border Inn in this charming village marks the terminus of the northbound Way, and it therefore follows that the ascending roadway directly

The summit of The Schil.

Following the Pennine Way to The Schil.

opposite must be the southbound route, which, of course, it is. But you may be forgiven on your first visit if you stand there and indulge in a moment's doubt.

Anyway, begin up the road leading away from the Border Inn as it ascends to cross a minor ridge, albeit a splendid undulating ridge originating on The Curr and worthy of exploration, containing as it does the remains of a fort on Wildgoose Hill. As you reach a cattle grid (840276) leave the road to ford Halter Burn to gain a broad track passing across the southern slopes of Green Humbleton, around which the tempting shape of Coldsmouth Hill looms into view. Soon you will encounter a gated fence giving access to England for the short stretch to the col between White Law and its minor acolyte. Another gate here takes you back into Scotland for a fine, airy traverse across The Curr col and back into England at the head of Fleehope Burn for the final assault on a summit which springs into view, most impressively, as you approach the col. The craggy outcrops, rocky topknot, and fringe of scree which decorate The Schil make it a most attractive mountaintop, while its distance from higher summits endows it with a fine panorama of tempting hills and an uninterrupted prospect to the North Sea and Scottish lowlands.

DISTANCE: 8.5 kilometres (5.3 miles)
ASCENT: 615 metres (2015 feet)

If returning to Kirk Yetholm divert as you approach The Curr col to a gate on the col, and descend beyond it to the head of the Halterburn valley, as if making for Latchly Hill (which, of course, you might be!). Beneath Latchly Hill the path splits again, one track leading down into Curr Burn and on to Primsidemill, while the 'Alternative' Pennine Way drops quickly to the ruins of Old Halterburn Farm where it continues easily via Burnhead and Halterburn back to the cattle grid encountered on the ascent. This alternative section of the Pennine Way, rather like its equivalent at the other end in Edale, is intended for poor weather. Given the extreme conditions of terrain and distances involved at both ends of the Pennine Way, my advice, faced with poor weather, is find the nearest pub and put your feet up until tomorrow!

Route 1.5 Windy Gyle Viewed over the top of Bloody-bush Edge from Cushat Law, Windy Gyle (855152) appears as a mere flattened mound of no significance, yet it is the focal point of a number of most rewarding excursions, some beginning in England, others in Scotland. And, of course, it lies on the Pennine Way, which in my view is only rewarding in bits – this is one of them! Essentially it is the approaches to Windy Gyle that form the attraction rather than the mountain itself, which is indeed a flattened mound. But seen from Hindside Knowe above Rowhope Burn it has a bold, dominating profile.

The summit lies in Scotland, and for the single stretch of ground along the Windy Gyle ridge so, too, does the Pennine Way. At either end of the ridge the Way skips back into England. I must confess, however, to a certain lack of conviction on this point. Careful examination on the ground reveals tell-tale signs of an earlier fenceline, and these are in places some distance removed from the

The summit of Cushat Law: Hedgehope Hill and The Cheviot rise in the background.

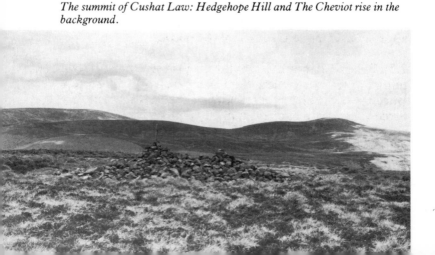

modern fence. The occasional old fence-post on the old line prompts me to speculate that this marks the true border.

The highest point of Windy Gyle, however, is not in doubt. A massive cairn, surmounted by a trig point and a star-shaped marker, is conspicuous for some distance. This is Russell's Cairn, named, it is claimed, after Lord Francis Russell, though the claim may be false. In mid-1585, when the Border troubles were at their height, Sir Thomas Kerr of Ferniehurst, Scotland, and Sir John Forster of England took their places at a Warden's Court somewhere high on the border ridge to deal with complaints and offenders from both sides of the border. Lord Francis Russell, Forster's son-in-law, was also present though he was the object of a grudge nursed by Kerr over the matter of the interception of coded messages. During the meeting a disturbance broke out among some by-standers which Russell attempted to quell, and for his pains received a bullet in the chest from which he died. Whether the killing was accidental or contrived is not clear, though subsequently Kerr was removed from his wardenship. In commemoration of the incident some of Russell's soldiers are said to have built a cairn at the place where he died, hence Russell's Cairn. Dispute, however, surrounds even this tantalising snippet of border history, for there is evidence to date the cairn to prehistoric, probably Bronze Age, times. Windy Gyle can be approached from either side of the border.

1.5a From Rowhope From the English side there is room to park a few cars where the River Coquet and Rowhope Burn meet, and from here, now a Land Rover track, The Street, once an ancient highway, provides a splendid ascent to the border ridge. The route is never in doubt as it ascends steadily over a succession of minor summits to join the Pennine Way a short way east of Mozie Law. From here a good track continues across Windy Rig before tackling a short pull to the top of Windy Gyle.

Much of the ground to the south and west as you ascend falls within the Otterburn Artillery Ranges and Training Area, and sections of The Street cross uncleared ground. Warning flags are flown whenever there is activity on the ranges, which seems to be most of the time. In the circumstances it is wise to observe the warning signs about picking up things "which may explode and kill you".

From the summit of Windy Gyle continue north-eastwards, towards The Cheviot, following the fenceline to the Border Gate at 871160. Here the ridge is crossed by another ancient highway, Clennell Street, which, if followed southwards, will bring you into the Usway valley near Hepden Burn. The return along the track to Trows and on to Rowhope Burn is all downhill and delightful.

DISTANCE: (Round trip) 15 kilometres (9.4 miles)
ASCENT: 385 metres (1260 feet)

1.5b From Calroust From Calroust, the track end on the Scottish side (824192), follow the path along the line of Calroust Burn as far as Calroust Hopehead where it arcs eastward before heading south again to ascend Windy Rig. This is a delightful and infrequently used approach, and well worth the effort of getting to Calroust.

DISTANCE: 6 kilometres (3.75 miles)
ASCENT: 400 metres (1310 feet)

1.5c From Cocklawfoot Like the ascent from Calroust the approach to Windy Gyle from Cocklawfoot in the Bowmont valley is little used. There are two lines, one ascending via Kelsocleugh, through the small plantation and on to Kelsocleugh Rig along a good path to Windy Rig, and the other from Cocklawfoot on an ascending path, passing between two small plantations and along the Cock Law ridge to the Border Gate. This latter route is the continuation of Clennell Street, and at 5.5 kilometres (3.4 miles) is one kilometre (0.6 miles) longer than the route to Windy Rig. The ascent in both cases is 380 metres (1245 feet).

Hedgehope Hill from Cushat Law.

Walkers seeking a long day in these fine hills should consider starting at Rowhope Burn, ascending The Street to Windy Gyle, then retracing their steps to descend Windy Rig to Cocklawfoot, returning to the Border Gate and the Usway valley along Clennell Street.

DISTANCE: 22 kilometres (13.75 miles)
ASCENT: 765 metres (2510 feet)

In spite of a prominent military presence this is unspoiled, untamed countryside at its best. Birds and animals are around in good numbers and long stretches of the border ridge are speckled in spring by the singular white flowers of cloudberry and in autumn by their orange berries. To set against this idyllic scene, distances in bad weather have that Scottish-mile feel about them, just that little bit further, and help or shelter is invariably a long way off.

Route 1.6 Bloodybush Edge Owning neither an edge, as walkers reared on granite or gritstone might envisage, nor sanguinary shrubbery, Bloodybush Edge (902143) perches alongside its companion, Cushat Law, in a raised semicircle of mountain moorland embracing the Kidland

Forest. Route 1.7 describes the means by which these two summits may be conveniently linked, but walkers seeking a shorter day will find the ascent from Uswayford to their taste.

Uswayford, a remote habitation, stands as its name suggests at a crossing of the Usway Burn in a wild cradle among the hills. The mere act of reaching Uswayford whether on foot or by car is a challenge in itself, taking the walker into the most beautiful of inner sanctums, Upper Coquetdale – a valley to rival any in the Pennines and many in Lakeland or across the border in Scotland.

Motorists will find that beyond Trows (855125) the road becomes a broad, graded track, still motorable but less tolerant of the deficiencies of modern transport. Walkers wanting an extended walk are advised to leave cars at the confluence of the River Coquet and the Rowhope Burn (859115) where there is ample space, and to follow the valley trail leisurely to Uswayford. The Usway Burn, it should be noted, although joined in its upper reaches actually enters Upper Coquetdale much lower down the valley, at Shillmoor.

From Uswayford take the rising path ascending to the col between Yarnspath Law and Bloodybush Edge, and then follow a fenceline (and an intermittent

Hedgehope Hill.

footpath) to the summit, marked by a trig point.
DISTANCE: (From Uswayford) 1.8 kilometres (1.1 miles)
ASCENT: 250 metres (820 feet)

The walk-in from the confluence will add 5.5 kilometres
(3.4 miles) each way.

The continuation to Cushat Law simply follows a fenceline roughly eastwards, leaving it for a dilapidated fence
as you approach the summit. There is however no convenient return from Cushat Law to Upper Coquetdale
beyond retracing one's steps. The grassy summit of
Yarnspath Law will provide a temporary diversion, facili-
tating a return to the valley road near Hepden Burn.

Route 1.7 Cushat Law Cushat Law (928137) is a fine,
grassy dome, like its neighbour, Bloodybush Edge,
caught between opposing ranks of Forestry Commission
conifers. The forest, however, does nothing to detract
from (and much to enhance) the general air of peaceful
contentment that settles on the walker bound this way on a
fine spring day, and the view provided of the higher
summits, The Cheviot and Hedgehope Hill, to the north is
second to none. Kidland Forest and its many trails provide the key to the ascent of Cushat Law, easing you up the

The summit of Windy Gyle.

Approaching Windy Gyle.

mountain's lower slopes almost effortlessly. The valley approaches from Ingram (018163) and Alnham (995109), passing around Shill Moor and followed by an easy ascent of grassy moorland, have their own charm, and are excellent alternative lines into this attractive region. The route from the south, however, along the River Alwin, is a more rewarding experience, especially for anyone venturing into the Cheviots for the first time, Clennell Hall (929071) proving an ideal base and offering ample accommodation whether residential, camping, caravanning or in neat self-contained chalets.

Without proper authority cars should not venture beyond the forest boundary (920092), and walks are calculated to start from there, though it is feasible to drive a good way into the forest. The walk-in, however, is not unattractive, and with sufficient time available, is to be preferred.

Follow the forest track along Yoke Burn, taking the right branch (below Heigh) heading towards Cushat Law. The name means 'the hill of the woodpigeons', and the forest provides shelter for a good number of them.

Eventually, after much to-ing and fro-ing (the map is quite accurate), you break free of the forest to arrive at a gate just beneath the summit, from where a short uphill pull across trackless ground will place you on top in a matter of minutes. The highest point is marked by a large cairn, just north of a line of dilapidated fence-posts, and beyond which, in a slight hollow, stands a large circular mound surmounted by a pole, within what appears to be a ring of stone footings. The view northwards is quite splendid.

DISTANCE: 6 kilometres (3.75 miles)
ASCENT: 405 metres (1330 feet)

The continuation to Bloodybush Edge follows the dilapidated fenceline until it meets a more substantial one, the various bends of which may be safely followed all the way to the summit. The going is a little damp underfoot.

DISTANCE: 3 kilometres (1.9 miles)
ASCENT: 115 metres (380 feet)

Walkers returning to the starting point, having extended their trek to Bloodybush Edge, should re-enter the forest along the footpath (896139 – shown on the 1:50 000 map) ascending from Uswayford, keeping above the line of trees

Approaching the summit of Windy Gyle.

The summit of Lamb Hill looking towards Beefstand Hill.

until a convenient firebreak allows you to descend to a broad forest trail (not shown on the map) leading you to the vicinity of Sneer Hill from where a descent may be made either to White Burn or Lindhope Burn, followed by an easy walk-out.

Route 1.8 Mozie Law, Beefstand Hill and Lamb Hill
These three relatively minor summits share themselves equally between Scotland and England, and though superficially uninteresting form a fine focal point for delightful, meandering excursions from both sides of the border. South of the border ridge the hills and moors sprawl massively, stretching out as if to make room for themselves, and contrast sharply with the northern side, where a pattern of tight little valleys and hummocky ridges tumble and twist towards the Tweed. The key to ascents to this short section of the Pennine Way is The Street, the ancient track linking Upper Coquetdale and the distant village of Hownam.

1.8a From Upper Coquetdale This approach to Mozie Law (829150) and company begins where the River Coquet and Rowhope Burn meet, and follows a prominent

Land Rover track shooting briskly up the lower slopes of Hindside Knowe (as described in Route 1.5a). The ascent is most pleasing, and the direction never in doubt, passing over a number of minor bumps before tackling Black Braes and the final pull to the border ridge. The views, certain on a good day to draw the attention constantly, simply get better as you gain height. The line of the border between Beefstand Hill and Windy Gyle does not always keep to the highest ground and here contorts to a childish squiggle with no apparent reason. But on breasting Black Braes the border fence on one of its forays into England is soon encountered, and may be followed left for a brief ascent to the top of Mozie Law, marked by an old Pennine Way marker, one of many originally erected by the Ramblers' Association.

Continue south and east along the fenceline to Beefstand Hill, and on and down to Lamb Hill, some of the roughnesses and wet spots between the two being avoided by resorting to short stretches of boardwalks. The trig on Lamb Hill stands in Scotland, while the highest points of Beefstand Hill and Mozie Law may be said to be equally divided.

From Lamb Hill descend due south over rough ground to intersect the path crossing Yearning Law, and continue down to Blindburn for an easy return along the minor road.

DISTANCE: (Round trip) 15.5 kilometres (9.7 miles)
ASCENT: 385 metres (1265 feet)

1.8b From Hownam The Street continues northwards from the border ridge to the picturesque village of Hownam (779193), and the ascent from this direction, not much visited by walkers, is quite delightful.

Begin by ascending a prominent track opposite the last house on the right, and climb to a large white house (initially obscured) on the hillside. Through a gate turn right along the line of The Street which throughout almost its entire length is easy to follow. A moment of doubt,

Approaching Black Braes on the ascent of The Street.

however, occurs quite early on, crossing Windy Law, where the regular use of tracks by farmers has given greater prominence to the wrong route. Keep your eyes open for a gate on the left, beyond which the way will be seen running alongside a wall and heading for Craik Moor, an obvious large lump on the left.

In springtime the valley slopes are dotted everywhere with the purple and yellow of wild and mountain pansies, and this wild region is popular with breeding wheatear, curlew, meadow pipit, skylark and lapwing. As you cross Craik Moor the hillfort on Blackbrough Hill is quite conspicuous, and may be reached easily by a short diversion. This whole region contains many such hillforts, built before, during and after the Roman presence; this one is a particularly good example and commands a fine view down the attendant valley.

At the head of Singingside Burn the track bends left to pass through a couple of gates before continuing its upward march to the border. As you approach the ridge, Windy Gyle ahead and The Cheviot and The Schil prominent in the distance, another track ascends from your right via Heatherhope Burn, and this is a speedy way down

Ascending The Street from Rowhope.

Ascending from the north to Windy Gyle and Mozie Law.

in the event of a sudden change in the weather; it is also an alternative and equally delightful way up!

Once on the border ridge cross into England and follow the fence (on your right) on to Mozie Law, Beefstand Hill and Lamb Hill, as described above. This has been a longer approach than from Coquetdale, and walkers wishing to save two kilometres or so should omit the trek to and from Lamb Hill and descend right towards the very tall cairn on Thorny Hill (Callaw Cairn) instead. There is a gate at the bend at 815141, beyond which a fence may be followed – the path is not very clear here – to join a better path on the east side of Thorny Hill. Head for the distant wall running towards Green Hill, and continue down to another hillfort at 796169. The path is not always clear along this section, but the going is easy, the direction never in doubt, and the route as marked on the map. The path finally emerges at Greenhill Farm, with a gentle return to Hownam along the minor road.

DISTANCE: (Round trip): 19 kilometres (11.9 miles)
ASCENT: 510 metres (1675 feet)

The track to Uswayford.

Route 1.9 Peel Fell from Kielder Peel Fell (626997) is
the highest of the afforested summits south of Redesdale,
and is ideal for a short day or winter excursion. It lies, too,
on a broad moorland ridge stretching to Carter Bar and on
to the foothills of the main Cheviot group north of Redesdale, the complete traverse of which, from Kielder, is a
fine undertaking.

The ascent to Peel Fell begins uneventfully enough
across a bridge over Deadwater Burn, leaving the minor
road between Kielder and Saughtree at 622946. The
ensuing track immediately branches, the left fork taking
you towards the edge of the forest ahead. Some sections of
the forest have been cleared, but the tracks remain and
should be followed in broad zig-zag sweeps until you
finally break free of the forest and can head directly for the
summit of Deadwater Fell. This summit is not a pretty
sight, its top cluttered with a proliferation of small buildings and masts.

A squishy path descends Deadwater Moor and on to
Mid Fell, on which there is a large cairn-shelter, with a fine

Peel Fell.

view across the many minor tops of the Kielder Forest region, and of the high moorland traverse to Carter Bar. A dilapidated fenceline guides you unerringly along a path and on in turn to the final slopes of Peel Fell. The summit has two points of equal height; one is marked by a large cairn, while the other occurs at the border fence.

DISTANCE: 7.5 kilometres (4.7 miles)
ASCENT: 485 metres (1590 feet)

Walkers needing to return to the start are faced either with retracing their steps, or continuing for a short distance across the top of Peel Fell to the border fence, and following this down towards Deadwater Burn. Again some of the forest has been cleared, and as you descend two options appear. One is to head left, to the top of Deadwater Burn, to gain the forest trails, all of which will return you to the start. The second option, more interesting, but more arduous, is to stay with the border fence until it finally reaches the metalled road at 603973, returning along the road from there. This option, however, takes you into some badly rutted and overgrown terrain, initially between opposing ranks of spruce. But in due course the going becomes more difficult as the trees close in, necessitating some to-ing and fro-ing across the border fence and an overgrown wall alongside it. Fallen branches and forestry debris do nothing to aid progress, and your final emergence from the forest will no doubt elicit a sigh of relief. If ever in doubt, stay with the fence.

The complete round trip, following the border fence for the final leg and returning along the road, covers 14.5 kilometres (9 miles).

Route 1.10 Carter Fell The few straggling summits stretching south-westwards along the border from Carter Bar are of little attraction in themselves, being for the most part flattish, frequently wet, and with few landmarks or local features of interest. They do however form a vital link for anyone contemplating the traverse of this most bloody and turbulent section of the border between the two countries, and anyone satisfied with wandering aimlessly (as it might seem) will find these modest heights good companions.

The ascent to the first summit, Carter Fell, a double-topped whale of a hill, is short and sharp, a feature for once likely to prove a welcome relief, especially in summer, when the border crossing is cluttered with cars, caravans, motor coaches, and the like, and throbs to the sound of querulous tourists and wailing bagpipes.

Carter Bar is a breathtaking spot and doesn't deserve all the clamour it receives. But, alas, it cannot avoid it, being by far the steepest and wildest highway across the border. Predictably, in winter it often becomes blocked with snow, not that that did more, it seems, than inconvenience that famous Newcastle–Edinburgh coach, The Chevy Chase, which crossed by this route in the early 1800s. If on your ascent of Carter Fell you divert to sit beside the prominent large cairn at the head of Black Cleugh and gaze down the valley towards Catcleugh Reservoir you cannot fail to be impressed by the tenacity of anyone organising or travelling on a passenger service across such lonely and isolated terrain. The horses must have possessed formidable strength to tackle a gradient that some cars have

Kielder Castle.

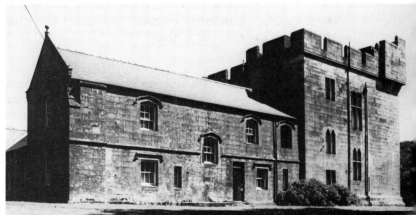

difficulty with even now, and the passengers a good deal more tolerance than their modern counterparts. Sadly, by the mid-1840s, when the link between the English and Scottish railways was completed at Berwick, the coach service had declined to oblivion.

Along the border now runs the customary fence, though there are frequently two, side by side, as if dispute still reigns over where, precisely, the border lies. Follow this fence from Carter Bar, initially alongside the forest, and up the short steep pull of Catcleugh Shin. An easier gradient is soon reached, leaving you with a gentle, if frequently wet, traverse of easy ground spotted in summer with the white flags of bog cotton to the trig marking the summit; a lonely and windswept top.

DISTANCE: 2.3 kilometres (1.4 miles)
ASCENT: 160 metres (525 feet)

The continuation to Carlin Tooth, Hartshorn Pike and Peel Fell initially stays with the border over Carter Fell's second top and on to the col at the head of Black Burn. Here the border is left, not to be regained until the summit of Peel Fell. The going throughout is much the same, and easiest to traverse after prolonged dry weather or when the ground is frozen. Only in mist is there likely to be any question over direction, but the boundary of the Wauchope Forest is always a reliable fail-safe.

Section 2 – The Northern Moors

	MAP REFERENCE	HEIGHT (m)	1:50 000 OS MAP
Cross Fell and Mickle Fell			
Cross Fell	687343	893	91
Great Dun Fell	710322	848	91
Little Dun Fell	704330	842	91
Knock Fell (Green Fell)	722303	794	91
Mickle Fell	804243	788	91/92

Meldon Hill	772291	767	91
Burton Fell	781223	748	91
(Hilton Fell)			
(Little Fell)			
Melmerby Fell	652380	709	91
Unnamed summit	726277	698	91
(Backstone Edge)			
Round Hill	744361	686	91
Cronkley Fell	843252	686	91
(Long Crag)			
Murton Fell	754246	675	91
Fiend's Fell	643406	634	86
Tynehead Fell	763350	620c	91
(Bellbeaver Rigg)			
Long Fell	768200	620c	91
Bink Moss	875243	619	91/92
Gilderdale			
Black Fell	648444	664	86
Grey Nag	665476	656	86
Tom Smith's Stone	655467	637	86
Thack Moor	611463	609	86
(Renwick Fell)			
Watch Hill	628460	602	86
(Graystone Edge)			
Blotting Raise	597495	591	86
Croglin Fell	615489	567	86
Geltsdale			
Cold Fell	606556	621	86
Great Blacklow Hill	622533	595	86
Three Pikes	634513	584	86
Tees and Wear			
Burnhope Seat	788375	746	91
Scaud Hill	795363	718	91
Dead Stones	794399	710c	86/91
Great Stony Hill ?	824359	708	91/92
Chapelfell Top	876346	703	91/92
(Langdon Fell)			
Fendrith Hill	877333	696	91/92
Outberry Plain	923326	675	91/92
Killhope Law	819448	673	86/87
Three Pikes	834343	651	91/92

Herdship Fell	789332	649	91
Flinty Fell	(771420 ★ (771442 ?	614	86/87
The Dodd	791458	614	86/87
Burtree Fell	862432	612	87
Carrs Hill (Racketgill Head)	947311	608	91/92
Black Hill	873411	604	87

★ Two summits of equal height 270 metres apart

ROUTES

Cross Fell from the east.

The mountain uplands which gather in that vague river-bound region north of the Dales but not so far north as the Cheviot Hills are too ill-defined to have acquired any true generic name. Most walkers recognise the eminence of Cross Fell and its acolytes, and names like Cauldron Snout, High Force, Teesdale and Weardale are sufficient to place the locality, roughly at least, in people's minds. But Geltsdale? East and West Allen? Dead Stones? Blotting Raise? – where (or what) are these?

The truth is, of course, they are all part of the Northern Moors; not an original name, but adequate to fill the gap, so to speak. The area comprising these northern moors is large and fragmented, hence the tendency for most walkers to recognise the juicy bits and wonder about the rest.

By way of reference, the area is bounded on the west by the broad Eden valley, a flat, pastoral plain keeping the Lakeland mountains and the M6 motorway at bay, and to the north the A69, or Hadrian's Wall, if you prefer. The

The western slopes of Cross Fell.

eastern boundary is roughly defined by Weardale, but includes the summits along the Durham/Northumberland border, while the southern connection lies through the Stainmore Gap, a traditional trans-Pennine link used by the Romans.

Within this (relatively) unknown area, surprisingly, is the largest concentration of hills in England outside the Lake District, culminating in the monarch of the Pennines, Cross Fell. And a great wedge of it has recently been designated an Area of Outstanding Natural Beauty. The reality may be that walkers are not so uninformed about this region as I might suppose. But many months of wandering there forced me into the company of others only in well-known areas; the whole of the area north of Hartside Cross, the South Tyne summits, and those along the borders with Durham and Northumberland, my companions and I toured alone.

Cross Fell is almost central to a long, undulating ridge of mountains which runs north—west from Brough in the south to the isolated northern summit of Cold Fell looking down on Brampton and the River Irthing. The further east you go the lesser are the mountains both in altitude and mass, until, around Weardale, you can romp up and down some in a matter of minutes. There is a stark contrast, too, between the lush valley of the Eden and the tilted, boggy moorland east of Cross Fell. It may be tempting to dismiss these moors as unappetising fare enriched only by the occasional taste of something more spicy. High Cup Nick, for example, is a fine moment of drama: a vast, elongated bowl rimmed with the shattered crags of the Whin Sill. Cauldron Snout, too, is fine recompense for Cow Green's greedy gulping of the Tees, though the reservoir, in spite of the botanical furore which greeted its construction, has assumed a naturalness quite remarkable for man's meddling. But, in the right mood, and on the right day, the surrounding bleakness betrays a subtlety of flavour hidden from all but the most perceptive palates; a soft, insinuating quality to make you smile inwardly as you battle with the bogs, or wander about mesmerised by the aimless wreaths of mist.

It has been said that in the Northern Moors it is the valleys rather than the hills which form the attraction, and this may be true. But no walker should turn his or her back on these moorland hills without closer acquaintance first. Troubles you will have in plenty, for distances are often long and the going tough, but the rewards are just and well earned.

Some parts of the region are affected by access controls. The massive sprawl of land around Mickle Fell, for example, is part of the Warcop Military Training Area (even though some of it is privately owned), stretching from Cronkley Fell in the north-east to the A66 in the south-west. The use made of the land by the military authorities tells you something about its nature. On the other hand, another large area nearby forms the Upper Teesdale National Nature Reserve, which tells you something else.

The Northern Moors are truly a remarkable and captivating chunk of the Pennines, too big to ignore, too wild to
take for granted. And I like to think it was more than mere
deference to the highest Pennine summit which caused the
originators of the Pennine Way to inject into this section a
massive loop, twice crossing the region at its most isolated
and highest points before resuming a more sedentary
course along the South Tyne.

Route 2.1 Cross Fell Lying "like a wall of brass", to
quote Daniel Defoe, along the eastern edge of Westmorland, the Pennines draw to their greatest height at the very
spot where the River Tees begins its long journey to the
North Sea. Overlooking the massively broad Eden valley,
a far cry from the pastoral loveliness sandwiched between
Wild Boar Fell and Mallerstang Edge where the Eden
rises, the highest summits of the Pennines form a seemingly impenetrable barrier between the Land of the
Lakes, which had commanded rather more of Mr. Defoe's
attention, and the moorlands of Cumberland and Westmorland and what was the North Riding of Yorkshire.

A casual study of the map suggests that Cross Fell
(687343), indisputably the highest of the Pennines and
once thought to boast even greater height, promises only
long and tedious walks of little interest. But nothing could
be further from the truth. Only the flat, bleak, windswept
summit plateau disappoints, and the arrival here of
walkers who have trudged from Edale or Kirk Yetholm
along the Pennine Way must evince an awful anticlimax –
could the summit not contrive at least one crowning
upthrust of rock, something a little more idealistically
pyramidal than the great rounded mound we find when its
seemingly perpetual cap of slowly moving cloud finally
exposes the summit for all to see? Nevertheless, Cross Fell
is, in truth, an imposing mountain, simple of line and
structure, but offering the walker a splendid selection of
ascents, well worthy of its status.

In fine weather, Cross Fell looks a calm, endearing place

to visit, but its repertoire of dirty tricks include sub-zero temperatures on at least a third of the days of the year, rain on two-thirds, and snow often well into summer. If that isn't enough, its *pièce de résistance* is a phenomenon known as the Helm wind, a remarkably ferocious and localised gusting of the wind. It is neatly summarised in *Legends and Historical Notes of North Westmoreland* by Thomas Gibson (1887): "the air or wind from the east [sic], ascends the gradual slope of the western side of the Pennine chain . . . to the summit of Cross Fell, where it enters the helm or cap, and is cooled to a less temperature; it then rushes forcibly down the abrupt declivity of the western side of the mountain into the valley beneath, in consequence of the valley being of a warmer temperature, and this constitutes the Helm-Wind. The sudden and violent rushing of the wind down the ravines and crevices of the mountain, occasions the loud noise that is heard." As for its strength, Thomas Wilkinson of Yanwath, a Quaker friend of Wordsworth, describes in his *Tour to the British Mountains* (1824), how "if I advanced it was with my head inclined to the ground, and at a slow pace; if I retreated and leaned against it with all my might, I could hardly keep erect; if I did not resist it, I was blown over."

Small wonder then that Cross Fell's original name was Fiends' Fell, before St. Augustine (it is claimed) erected a cross on its summit, built an altar to celebrate the Holy Eucharist in order to scatter the resident devils. Camden thought it was "an extraordinary piece of devotion . . . to erect Crosses and build Chapels in the most eminent places, as being both nearer Heaven and more conspicuous". If any demons remained in the face of such overwhelming Christianity there is a good chance they finally took flight when, in days when political fervour was greater than it is today, some fifty brass bands gathered on the summit to celebrate the passing of the Reform Act of 1832.

In spite of its unappealing summit plateau and the high incidence of clouds which bedevil the mountain, Cross

The two Dun Fells: Little and Great.

Great Dun Fell from Cross Fell.

Fell is a superb viewpoint, taking in the fells of Lakeland dotting the horizon beyond the Eden valley, and extending far across the northern counties, into Scotland.

Daniel Defoe's comment about the Pennines being like a wall of brass was close to the truth for they formed the mainstay of a substantial industry in the extraction of lead ore. Cross Fell may look solid, but it is honeycombed by shafts and levels that contributed to a total yield, primarily during the eighteenth and nineteenth century, of over 3 million tons from the North Pennine fields alone. Nor was lead the only mineral to be won. From 1725 to 1870 the amount of silver refined from lead, in the areas of the North Pennines, was approximately 5.5 million ounces. Clearly the lead mining industry made a very great economic contribution to the country, until cheaper supplies from abroad seriously affected home production, and Cross Fell had its own part to play.

Walkers undertaking the Pennine Way will find the day that includes Cross Fell a long one. If they stay overnight in Dufton, as is normal, they must then begin a long ascent taking in Knock Fell, Great Dun Fell and Little Dun Fell before even setting foot on the mountain. And as they leave it behind, they face another long journey to reach Garrigill, or more usually Alston, before nightfall. Such a traverse is undoubtedly a rewarding, if arduous, one, and the ascent from either Dufton or Garrigill is, for walkers not tackling the Way, well worth undertaking. Shorter in length, but no less acceptable, are ascents from Knock, Blencarn, Kirkland and Townhead, while that from the summit of the Penrith–Alston road, at Hartside Cross, also takes in other summits before reaching Cross Fell.

2.1a From Dufton This is the approach taken by the Pennine Way, and the descriptions contained in Routes 2.2 and 2.3 will bring you to Little Dun Fell, from where a short descent north-westward places you at Tees Head, the birthplace of the River Tees. Beyond, a clear track ascends the scree slopes of Cross Fell to a number of cairns, including one very tall one, on the edge of the summit plateau, and from here it is a short stroll (but a potentially confusing one in mist) to the summit trig and its attendant stone shelter.

DISTANCE: (Via Knock Fell) 12.3 kilometres (7.7 miles)
ASCENT: 910 metres (2985 feet)
DISTANCE: (By Great Dun Fell direct) 11.7 kilometres (7.3 miles)
ASCENT: 860 metres (2820 feet)

2.1b From Knock The ascent from Knock is, if you want it to be and providing you have a car, by far the easiest and shortest ascent of Cross Fell. The key to this accomplishment is the motorable roadway, originally a mine road, but now extended to service the radar station on the summit of Great Dun Fell, which leaves the minor road north of Knock at 676274. Route 2.2 reveals all.

DISTANCE: 11 kilometres (6.9 miles)
ASCENT: 815 metres (2675 feet)

2.1c From Blencarn Blencarn is a neat, attractive village, largely minding its own business, and a superb place from which to watch the rays of a setting sun bathe the distant slopes of Cross Fell. From the southern end of the village a signposted track (640312) leads first to Wythwaite, and then to a path courting the beck which drains from Wildboar Scar. Continue along the path as it crosses and ascends the Scar until a gently sloping plateau is reached with the scree slopes of Cross Fell beyond, and good views of the two Dun Fells.

A narrow, cairned path now makes for Tees Head, though the path may be difficult to locate in poor visibility and at Tees Head becomes lost among the boulders and scree. From Tees Head turn from a northeasterly direction to a north-westerly to ascend the final scree slopes of the fell to the summit plateau.

DISTANCE: 7.6 kilometres (4.75 miles)
ASCENT: 715 metres (2345 feet)

This is a delightful approach, though better used as a descent following an ascent from Kirkland (Route 2.1d). The section between Wildboar Scar and Grumply Hill, following the course of the beck, is quite splendid.

The short stretch between Wythwaite and Kirkland follows a good track (shown on the map), and passes a curious feature known as the Hanging Walls of Mark Antony. Precisely what they are, or were, is open to doubt, and other than a series of mounds, claimed by some to be natural, there is little to see. The Maiden Way, a Roman road, is not too far away to the north, and this may have occasioned some fanciful thinking in years gone by. Certainly local inhabitants seem unimpressed, questioning whether Mark Antony ever ventured to Britain, and suggesting that the only thing Roman about the mounds is the name.

2.1d From Kirkland This ascent, used now by hang-gliders who power their heavily laden four-wheel drives up it to gain the heights of High Cap, is an old corpse road linking the church and graveyard at Kirkland with Garrigill. In the seventeenth century one funeral party is known to have abandoned its burden when caught in a blizzard high up on the mountainside, scurrying back to Garrigill, and returning only two weeks later for the coffin when it was finally considered safe to recover it. The mourners then brought the coffin back to Garrigill where it was buried in a piece of glebe land, subsequently consecrated by the Bishop of Durham as a burial ground.

The route is clear throughout, starting east along Kirkland Beck, and later curving north to skirt High Cap. As the gradient eases a few old pits are found, as the route continues easily eastwards on a cairned path, passing round the northern scree slopes of Cross Fell to locate and follow the Pennine Way on its hurried descent to Garrigill. On a clear day you could make for the summit as soon as you feel happy about it, if you have no objection to messing about on scree. But the line taken by the Pennine

Way is clear enough in all but the worst conditions and, though initially damp underfoot as it climbs away from the corpse road, it dries out as you gain height. A line of cairns steers you to the summit.

DISTANCE: 6.5 kilometres (4 miles)

ASCENT: 690 metres (2265 feet)

As suggested earlier, this ascent may be combined with a descent of Route 2.1c over Wildboar Scar, returning from Wythwaite via the Hanging Walls of Mark Antony. A thoroughly delightful proposition on a clear day, when the northern fells of Lakeland and the southern counties of Scotland across the Solway Firth form a distant frieze to the horizon.

2.1e From Townhead The small group of buildings that constitute Townhead could easily be ignored and passed by. But they stand on the line of an important Roman road, the Maiden Way, which ran from the fort (Bravoniacum) at Kirkby Thore over the fells to Alston and Carvoran on Hadrian's Wall. The Maiden Way may be followed quite easily, and in sections remains can still be found of the original Roman handiwork.

There is an imaginative suggestion that the Maiden Way was constructed to enable a princess from the south to ride to her marriage in Scotland without facing a ford deep enough to cause her bridal dress to be splashed with water. Just what condition the dress might have been in anyway following a journey on horseback of some days is something to wonder about; as, no doubt, would be the wisdom of marrying someone prepared even to contemplate such a journey, princess, or no princess!

The Maiden Way leaves Townhead along a minor track (635340) following Ardale Beck, and soon climbs steeply to Man at Edge. From there pass behind Muska Hill to make for a wall running beneath the escarpment edge ahead. The objective, though you need not go quite so far, is Meg's Cairn (657374), standing on the col between distant Cross Fell and Melmerby Fell. Just who Meg was is not clear. The horseriding princess bride, perhaps? Or the subject of some wall-builder's desire?

Once above the intake wall and on the escarpment it is a simple, if longish, walk to Cross Fell, joining the old corpse road en route, and following Route 2.1d to finish.
DISTANCE: 9 kilometres (5.6 miles)
ASCENT: 680 metres (2230 feet)

By combining Routes 2.1d and 2.1e you can provide yourself with a rewarding visit to the summit of Cross Fell by routes largely unused by walkers, and in a most attractive area.

2.1f From Hartside Cross Hartside Cross marks the highest point of the A686 Penrith–Alston road, a route often blocked by snow in winter, and it offers an alternative and long approach to Cross Fell passing first over the minor summit, Fiend's Fell, and Melmerby Fell.

The ascent to Melmerby Fell is contained in Route 2.10, and from that summit an easy descent may be made to Meg's Cairn where you join Route 2.1e (the Maiden Way) and later Route 2.1d (the old Corpse Road) to reach your objective.
DISTANCE: 9.5 kilometres (6 miles)
ASCENT: 390 metres (1280 feet)

2.1g By the Maiden Way from the A686 This is an unconventional approach to Cross Fell, suitable for walkers based in Alston, who might wish to return via Garrigill, and likely to appeal to people who like moorland solitude. The line taken follows the Maiden Way to Meg's Cairn where it joins routes previously described for the final section to Cross Fell summit. In the upper part of this walk, as it crosses the slopes of Melmerby Fell, there are a few partially exposed sections of what seems to be the original Roman road.

Begin down a walled track leaving the A686 at 677423 and where it bends right, turn left to follow a broad track heading to a small copse (shown on the map). Here the track bends and descends to Rowgill Burn, crossing it at a ford which could be a problem for walkers after heavy rain. Once across the burn the path ascends the moorland beyond, and is easy to follow. Where it turns abruptly to drop to Smittergill Head however you should keep ahead on a less well defined track, though it is occasionally cairned. This is the line of the Maiden Way, which in due course improves and brings you to Meg's Cairn. The rest of this approach is described in the preceding Route.

DISTANCE: 10 kilometres (6.25 miles)
ASCENT: 515 metres (1690 feet)

2.1h From Garrigill This is the final ascent of Cross Fell, and the line taken by the Pennine Way, usually in descent. Garrigill is a quiet hamlet strung along the South Tyne, in many ways a secluded backwater off the tourist routes (Pennine Wayfarers excepted), charmingly set around a village green.

The Pennine Way leaves the minor road through the valley at 746412 and follows a walled route on to Black Band Moor. The 1:50 000 map suggests a short cut, leaving the walled route and rejoining it later, but there is no advantage in this. In due course the path leaves first one wall and then the other behind as it passes by Pikeman Hill and Long Man Hill.

It will become obvious as you progress that you are entering a region that has seen a good deal of mining activity. In fact, you are approaching the remains of the Cashwell mine, one of the most productive in the Northern Pennines. As you go keep your eyes open for fragments of lead ore (galena), lumps of barytes, and yellow or blue fluorspar, the latter known in Derbyshire as Blue John, and claimed only to be found there!

The abandoned mines and their ruined buildings are of

great interest, but potentially dangerous, and care is needed in their vicinity.

This approach is well marked throughout, and eventually brings you to the edge of Cross Fell screes, for an ascent via Crossfell Well to the summit; this last uphill section being in common with the ascents from Kirkland, Townhead and Hartside.

DISTANCE: 11.5 kilometres (7.2 miles)
ASCENT: 550 metres (1805 feet)

Route 2.2 Great Dun Fell The building of a radar station on the summit of Great Dun Fell (710322) has made it one of the most unattractive mountaintops in Britain. It has also made it the most accessible, a former mine road up Knock Ore Gill having been metalled all the way to the summit, making this the highest motorable road in England, and the only one with the top of a mountain as its objective. Winter skiers find the road a major labour-saving device, but no self-respecting walker would drive up it . . . would they?

The summit, the second highest in the Pennines, lies south-east of Cross Fell, at the heart of the ancient Milburn Forest, with Little Dun Fell squatting between the two. It appears as a flattened mound, its white geodesic domes, teed up as if for some leviathan game of golf, visible for a considerable distance. The easiest line of ascent makes use of the road, though I commend this as a speedy descent, having first ascended the Pennine Way over Knock Fell (Route 2.3). To the east of the fell an old stony track, the remains of one of the London Lead Company's mine roads, strikes down to the head of Teesdale and on into South Tynesdale, and this provides a rather more demanding option.

Great Dun Fell and its 'Little' companion suffer much the same climatic problems as Cross Fell, the three summits together being the highest in the Pennines. Most walkers will embrace the three summits (or more) in one walk, indeed Pennine Wayfarers have no choice in the matter, and particular attention needs to be given to the importance of suitable protective clothing for a prolonged stay at a high and exposed altitude with little shelter. The summit lies, in fact, on the watershed of Britain, rain falling on the east side of the mountain flowing ultimately to the North Sea, while rainfall on the west finds its way into the Eden and the Irish Sea.

2.2a From Knock For the speediest approach simply follow the service road, which leaves the minor road north of Knock village at 676274. The ascent is not unpleasant,

Great Dun Fell.

and in the upper reaches of Knock Ore Gill the scenery quite fine, the summit ironmongery being briefly out of sight. The precise location of the highest point is debatable.

DISTANCE: 7.8 kilometres (4.9 miles)
ASCENT: 645 metres (2115 feet)

2.2b From Dufton An alternative approach from the west starts in Dufton, and pursues the Pennine Way either over Knock Fell, the new route avoiding Knock Ore Gill, or by the old route, which cuts across into the gill and follows the service road through the upper section. The former is detailed in Route 2.3.

At the northern end of Dufton village a signposted route follows the lane to Coatsike Farm, dominated by the fine cone of Dufton Pike. Beyond Coatsike the route follows a former access lane to Halsteads (691270 – shown, but not named on the 1:50 000 map). The lane, once beautiful, now suffers from the neglect of non-use, and has become wet and overgrown, forcing walkers to move further and further into the adjoining field to make reasonable progress.

A short way beyond Halsteads the path kinks around Cosca Hill, a minor projection of Dufton Pike, and descends a little to cross Great Rundale Beck by a quaint clapper bridge. Follow now the line of a stone wall (a second, dilapidated wall appearing on the right) to a gate, and eventually on to a signposted path slanting across the fellside to Knock Ore Gill. A much clearer, green path rises on your right here, and sends you haring off in error up High Scald Fell (the voice of experience), not that it matters much, but there is no right of way in this direction. If in doubt, remember that the Pennine Way ascends to Knock Fell along the north side of Swindale Beck, and that the track into Knock Ore Gill leaves the Pennine Way at the point where you cross Swindale Beck.

Once on the metalled roadway it is an easy finish to the summit.

DISTANCE: 8.4 kilometres (5.25 miles)
ASCENT: 680 metres (2230 feet)

2.2c Via Tyne Head Crossing the watershed separating the South Tyne and the Tees, an old mine road continues from the minor road extending southwards from Garrigill (758384). The track squeezes through a gap between Round Hill and Tynehead Fell, and descends to cross the Tees near an abandoned mine, continuing then along the north (true left) bank of Trout Beck to reach the col between Knock Fell and Great Dun Fell, from where the summit is but a short scamper away.
DISTANCE: (From Garrigill) 15 kilometres (9.4 miles)
ASCENT: 505 metres (1655 feet)

This approach passes through some very wild and remote countryside, and requires favourable conditions for a full and safe enjoyment.

The continuation from Great Dun Fell to Little Dun Fell (and from there to Cross Fell) is uncomplicated, if a trifle wet in stretches.

Descend from the northern perimeter fence of the radar station to a boggy col beyond which an easy pull places you on the summit of Little Dun Fell, the summit being marked by a cairn. The col beyond marks the former boundary between Cumberland and Westmorland (it's all in Cumbria now), and is the birthplace of the River Tees. A short ascent takes you through the ring of Cross Fell screes and on to the summit plateau.

Walkers wanting to return either to Knock or Dufton could consider contouring around Great Dun Fell on the return journey, by making first for the Silverband Mine, and using its service road to re-enter Knock Ore Gill in its upper section. This saves plodding back up and over Great Dun Fell.

Route 2.3 Knock Fell Knock Fell (722303) is unlikely to be the sole objective of a day's walking, having about it few of the qualities necessary to inspire such undivided attention. But given the right conditions an enjoyable excursion can be made over the fell which might include Meldon Hill or Backstone Edge. If it's solitude you want, however, a time of year when Pennine Wayfarers are thin on the ground is essential.

2.3a From Knock As is the case with Great Dun Fell the ascent of Knock Fell is made simple by the metalled roadway servicing the radar station on the former's summit, and this allows walkers to drive (Heaven forbid!) to the main Pennine watershed on the col between the two mountains. The summit of Knock Fell is then easily reached by a wet path ascending in an almost straight line to the large cairn marking the highest point.

For the purposes of calculating the following distance and ascent measurements it has been assumed that walkers will do the honourable thing and walk up, rather than drive.

DISTANCE: 7.7 kilometres (4.8 miles)
ASCENT: 590 metres (1935 feet)

2.3b From Dufton The ascent from Dufton involves using the Pennine Way, and the greater part of this approach is detailed in Route 2.2b. The two routes diverge at the crossing of Swindale Beck, with the Pennine Way (shown in black on the 1:50 000 map) plodding upwards along the north (true right) bank of the beck, and following a line of cairns. Ahead of you, and in view for some time, is Knock Old Man, a fine and well-constructed cairn a short distance from the less inspiring structure on the summit. In the upper reaches of Swindale Beck, however, you will first encounter Knock Hush, a man-made water channel, artificially created by releasing water dammed higher on the fellside. There are quite a number of hushes in the Pennines – there is another on the ascent of Great Dun Fell, for example – and they were used to scour away vegetation from underlying minerals, in this case lead.

The summit of Knock Fell has nothing about it to encourage you to linger. If it's shelter you want, you should push on a short way to some ruined huts on the descent to the col with Great Dun Fell.

DISTANCE: 6.5 kilometres (4 miles)
ASCENT: 620 metres (2035 feet)

2.3c Via High Scald Fell Knock Fell may also be reached from Dufton by a slightly longer, and equally interesting route. This takes the signposted route ('High Scald Fell') in the centre of Dufton and passes Dufton Pike on its south side. Shortly the route crosses towards Great Rundale Beck, and if you ever aspire to climb Dufton Pike, a commendable proposition, you can do so from this path.

For Knock Fell continue on the track you have been following into the upper reaches of Great Rundale Beck, pleasant enough if you concentrate your attention backwards rather than forwards to a rash of mine buildings and the spoil of old workings. Beyond the buildings the valley narrows as you approach the col between Backstone Edge and High Scald Fell, the highest point of the col being in the vicinity of Great Rundale Tarn, a delightful spot in an otherwise desolate setting. Turn left (north) here, and ascend easily to the summit of High Scald Fell, marked by a cairn, before striking out for Knock Fell.

DISTANCE: 7 kilometres (4.4 miles)
ASCENT: 610 metres (2000 feet)

2.3d Via Tyne Head An ascent of Knock Fell via Tyne Head from Garrigill is substantially detailed in Route 2.2c and requires only that on reaching the col between Great Dun Fell and Knock Fell you divert east of south to gain the wet path climbing easily to the summit.

DISTANCE: 15.7 kilometres (9.8 miles)
ASCENT: 450 metres (1475 feet)

An extension from Knock Fell to take in the remote summit, Meldon Hill, calls for considerable determination. Even a cursory study of the map will suggest that the proliferation of burns, sikes and becks can mean only one thing – water. 'Wet' is likely to be the best going you will encounter, swelling by degrees to 'impassable'. The line strikes first eastwards to a small tarn (736303), and gradually curves south-eastwards, calling for good navigational ability, not only because of the difficulty of the terrain, but also because Meldon Hill is not a conspicuous feature on this approach and can easily be missed in the vast spread of moorland.

DISTANCE: 5.3 kilometres (3.3 miles)
ASCENT: 65 metres (215 feet)

Route 2.4 Meldon Hill Meldon Hill (772291) stands east of the main Pennine ridge overlooking the collecting grounds of the Tees. It is a large, sprawling hill bedevilled by more than its fair share of bogs, without which it would be an attractive excursion from Dufton or Langdon Beck. As it is the conqueror of Meldon Hill must do battle with difficult terrain that will repulse other than the strongest walkers.

High Cup Nick.

High Cup Nick.

2.4a From Dufton Walkers ascending from Dufton must follow the Pennine Way as far as High Cup Nick, and this is described in detail in the route which follows (2.5 Backstone Edge). Suffice it to say that the journey to High Cup Nick is delightful, the onward trek to Meldon Hill less so.

In the vicinity of High Cup Nick you will encounter a signpost pointing to the bridge crossing Maize Beck (749270) at an interesting limestone gorge, and you should make for this. Once across the bridge press on upwards on a roughly north-easterly bearing to reach the trig and cairns which mark the summit. This is not easy going, and must not be tackled in poor visibility.

DISTANCE: 9.5 kilometres (6 miles)
ASCENT: 580 metres (1900 feet)

2.4b From Cow Green Reservoir Completed in 1970 the Cow Green Reservoir met with considerable opposition during construction because of the internationally re-

High Force, Teesdale. ▶

nowned status of the area especially for botanists. When the reservoir is full it has a splendidly wild and natural look about it, reminiscent of many remote parts of Scotland, but when the water is low the effects of man's interference are all too plainly evident and a sad memorial to a most beautiful region. As if by way of atonement the Nature Conservancy Council have carried out admirable work to concentrate public attention around Widdybank Fell, part of the Upper Teesdale National Nature Reserve, where a Nature Trail embellishes the walk to Cauldron Snout. Elsewhere access to the Reserve, which covers land in the ownership of the Earl of Strathmore and Lord Barnard, is less welcome, restricting walkers' freedom to wander at will to such public rights of way as exist.

From the car park (810309) follow the signs for Cauldron Snout as far as the dam of the reservoir. A diversion to examine Cauldron Snout, where the controlled waters of the Tees cascade over the Whin Sill, is well worthwhile. For Meldon Hill you need to cross the dam to gain the open hillside beyond. Any line taken from here to the summit will lead into difficult terrain, but the opening views across the reservoir and south to Mickle Fell provide

Falcon Clints, Maize Beck.

an element of compensation. There are no rights of way on to Meldon Hill.

DISTANCE: 6.8 kilometres (4.25 miles)
ASCENT: 280 metres (920 feet)

2.4c From Langdon Beck This approach to Meldon Hill is the longest, but it is most attractive. Follow the minor road leading to the reservoir, leaving it after a while for the track to Widdy Bank Farm which shelters beneath the imposing cliffs of Cronkley Scar. The scenery improves with every step as you now continue along a flat stretch of ground, Holmwath, and on to Falcon Clints. A little rough, bouldery going merely adds interest until finally you reach the confluence of Maize Beck, the onward line for Pennine Wayfarers, and the Tees at Cauldron Snout. This is the boundary between Cumbria and Durham, and, until local government reorganisation in 1974, between Westmorland, Durham and Yorkshire.

Round a corner the waters of the Tees throw themselves down the steps of the underlying Whin Sill in a spectacular display of natural force. A way can be found easily up the right-hand side (east) of the falls to a bridge beneath the dam walls. Go left across the bridge and follow the dam service road, right, to reach the edge of the dam wall, where you join and follow Route 2.4b above to the summit.

DISTANCE: 10.5 kilometres (6.6 miles)
ASCENT: 385 metres (1265 feet)

Route 2.5 Backstone Edge Backstone Edge (726277) is strictly a line of crags, especially noticeable from the vicinity of Dufton Pike, along the western edge of a high moorland plateau between High Scald Fell and High Cup Gill. The summit, an unnamed summit, has little merit, with low heather and tussock grass underfoot to impede rapid progress in those areas not already rendered desperate by bogs.

The confluence of the Tees and Maize Beck.

Not a pretty picture, perhaps; but for someone who wants to view High Cup Nick without having to return the same way the route that follows makes the effort of crossing three kilometres (about two miles) of difficult ground when all the rest is easy, worthwhile. Frozen ground makes for the best progress, though a dry summer day will also produce acceptable conditions for an interesting excursion. It should be noted, however, that while the lines of ascent and descent are public rights of way the intermediate ground, over Backstone Edge, is not.

The ascent starts from Dufton, a small cluster of cottages that probably would be totally unknown outside the immediate neighbourhood were it not for an idiosyncratic kink in the line of the Pennine Way, for here it quits the high ground to halt overnight before pressing on to the highest Pennine summit, Cross Fell, on what is a long day. Quite reasonably the designers of the Pennine Way considered the long haul from Teesdale more than a body can stand in one day and elected to alight upon the oasis of Dufton; Dufton, alas, seems to have been singularly unprepared for the invasion, and has, even now, limited accommodation possibilities, a feature which disposed the author of *The Pennine Way Companion*, Wainwright, to observe: "Wise virgins book their beds in advance." Which makes me wonder how many wise virgins pass along the Pennine Way.

Begin then along the signposted 'Pennine Way', at the southern end of the village. There is little opportunity to park nearby, though if you press on a little further into the village you should find somewhere unobtrusive. You will invariably find a red flag flying at the start of the Way. This signifies that firing is likely to occur on the Warcop Artillery Range – about which more in the entry for Murton Fell (Route 2.6) – but this route is entirely outside the range.

A good track leads away from Dufton, passing Bow Hall Farm, and continuing, via a few gates to the intake wall. The retrospective view here is especially rewarding, looking across the Eden valley to the fells of Lakeland. Just beyond the intake wall, up on the left, is a small shelter used in the days when there was a lime kiln nearby.

Continue now uneventfully along what is the edge of the escarpment dropping to High Cup Gill, though it is not immediately obvious. As you press on, however, the startling scenery of the upper gill becomes predominant and draws your eye quite forcefully, a spectacular outcropping of the Whin Sill basalts forming a huge bowl-shaped amphitheatre. The path keeps a respectable distance

On Backstone Edge. Snow-covered Mickle Fell rises in the background.

from the edge of the escarpment, but a visit to the edge is worthwhile at least once to view Nichol's Chair, a dramatic finger of basalt standing proud from the main edge of cliffs. It is named after a cobbler who used to live in Dufton, and who not only climbed the pillar but is reputed to have repaired a pair of boots while on its top.

The Pennine Way presses on eastward now to Teesdale, while for Backstone Edge you must about face, to ascend the easy slopes north-east of Narrowgate Beacon. Once on top you will encounter a trying section of bogs, giving way eventually to heather and tussock grass. Your objective is the trig pillar near the summit, en route to which you will pass a series of tarns, not always as easily found as you might expect since they lie at a slightly lower level than the highest ground for which one instinctively makes. In winter especially you can pass them by without ever seeing them. The highest point of this nondescript hill lies a short way north-east of the trig, and is marked by a cairn of large boulders.

DISTANCE: 8.4 kilometres (5.25 miles)
ASCENT: 510 metres (1675 feet)

Backstone Edge.

Continue from the summit to the col with High Scald Fell where you will encounter a good track leading west (left) to the head of Great Rundale Beck, and down to Dufton. There is a disused mine building a short way down the track, which makes a pleasant shelter, and shortly after this quarry workings are encountered, which, though having an air of neglect about them, are still evidently in use from time to time. Once beyond the workings the valley opens out, with a splendid view of Dufton Pike. Continue on a good, broad track, keeping south as you approach Dufton Pike, finally to reach Dufton not far from your starting point

DISTANCE: 6 kilometres (3.75 miles)

You can, of course, reverse this route, with equal acceptability.

Route 2.6 Murton Fell Murton Fell (754246) lies along the southern part of that great central ridge of the Pennines culminating in Cross Fell. Predictably, for it happens a number of times, the fell takes its name from the

Dufton Pike.

small cluster of buildings gathering at its feet and bearing the collective village name, Murton. Interest in the fell is minimal. Like most of these rounded, tussocky moorland hills it provides greatest sport for the walker in winter, especially if the walker also has an aptitude on skis. It is its use for a different sport, however, which places Murton Fell, and many more of these summits, in the extremely sensitive category, for they are wealthy and abundant grouse moors. Murton Fell, too, has yet another distinction, which summits further north do not; it lies on the edge of the Warcop Principal Training Area, in short, an artillery range. Firing on the artillery range takes place on every day except Mondays, and to indicate that the range is live, red warning flags are flown at strategic points around the perimeter of the range and at principal access points. Information about firing times is published in the *Cumberland and Westmorland Herald* monthly, about seven days before the end of the previous month. Further information may be obtained by ringing the Range Officer on Brough (09304) 661, who, more often than not, will tell you that firing will occur from O-nine hundred hours to seventeen hundred hours (ie nine to five in English) – which is an awful lot of banging!

Walkers intent on getting on to Murton Fell must first remind their consciences that it is private land and an active grouse moor, and then pursue Route 2.5 from Dufton as far as High Cup Nick. It is always difficult to know whether or not to venture on to known grouse moors: certainly it is wise to avoid the grouse-shooting season (roughly August–October), and for the rest of the year tread warily. From the top of High Cup Nick a steady ascent of the northern flank of Murton Fell will bring you first to a cairn-shelter beyond which, about one kilometre further across rather boggier ground than that encountered so far, the highest point stands unmarked. Neither of the spot heights shown on the 1:50 000 map is the summit; this lies about one-third of the way from the southern spot height to the northern, and is difficult to locate in mist.

DISTANCE: 7.5 kilometres (4.7 miles)
ASCENT: 485 metres (1590 feet)

An alternative approach may be made from Hilton, along the line of Hilton Beck. Unlike the ascent from Dufton, this approach lies within the artillery range, but is safe on Mondays! If you elect to continue the circuit over Murton Fell (returning along the minor road to Hilton), the advantage of this approach then lies in the way it brings you upon High Cup Nick quite dramatically, rather than the gradual build up you get climbing from Dufton. But both are extremely pleasant.

Route 2.7 Burton Fell Rejoicing also in the names of Hilton Fell, Little Fell (not on the 1:50 000 map) and Warcop Fell, Burton Fell (a name given slightly greater prominence by the Ordnance Survey, 781223) is a broad, wild moorland offshoot of Mickle Fell. It lies, alas, smack in the middle of the Warcop Artillery Range, and as such is only available to walkers on Mondays (see Route 2.6 for details); to make matters worse, these are also active grouse moors, which in some eyes denies them to walkers, *full stop!*

The simplest way of reaching Burton Fell is to follow the beautiful course of Hilton Beck, and, on escaping from the clutches of the valley, heading south-east across tussocky, untracked terrain for the highest ground, where the summit trig will be found enclosed in a circular stone wall, which effectively screens the trig from view until you reach it.

DISTANCE: 8.5 kilometres (5.3 miles)
ASCENT: 505 metres (1655 feet)

Route 2.8 Mickle Fell The ascent of Mickle Fell (804243), a long and desolate proposition from any direction, is plagued with difficulty, made worse by the mountain's obvious appeal when seen from adjacent and more northern summits. Firstly, it is within a large area of moorland owned and managed by the Strathmore Estate as active grouse moors. Secondly, it lies within the Warcop Artillery Range, with Mondays the only days when firing is claimed not to occur (see Route 2.6 for details). Thirdly, it lies within the Upper Teesdale National Nature Reserve, who are keen to ensure that the many natural habitats both for flora and fauna remain undisturbed.

Correspondence with the three interested parties produces a varied but emphatic response, the net effect of which is 'Keep Out'. The Strathmore English Estates are managed by Messrs. Arthur Young, Chartered Surveyors, of Newcastle-upon-Tyne, who, in pointing out the difficulties of access, indicate that the Estate "is content that walkers should use the existing footpaths when walking in this area of the Durham Dales." The Commanding Officer of the Warcop Training Area indicates that "We fire every day including weekends, except on Mondays on which day the public rights of way are of course open." He goes on to point out that a large part of the Training Area is private land, and so "the appropriate Landowner must be approached to obtain access where no right of way exists." The office of the Nature Conservancy Council at Forest-in-Teesdale responds: "Mickle Fell does not have footpaths. It is also part of the MOD area, which rules out access."

By way of a footnote to this saga of impenetrability it is interesting to note that during 1988 some 772 square miles of North Pennine landscape between Stainmore and South Tyne (and this includes the area around Mickle Fell) were declared an Area of Outstanding Natural Beauty, which, of course, it is. The Chairman of the Countryside Commission, commenting on the announcement, said: "We are keen that local people should get every opportunity to benefit and that visitors should get the maximum enjoyment." What a pity we can't get at it to enjoy it!

2.8a From Cow Green Reservoir The best ascent of Mickle Fell, though I hasten to add the going is far from easy, is from the banks of Maize Beck, approached from the Cow Green Reservoir car park (810309), by way of Cauldron Snout. This involves fording the beck at some stage, and should not be contemplated when the beck is in spate. An ascent roughly along the line of the county boundary will suffice to bring you to the large summit cairn marking the highest point.
DISTANCE: 8.5 kilometres (5.3 miles)
ASCENT: 355 metres (1165 feet)

2.8b From Teesdale A good track runs from Holwick (903271) to Silverband Shop (838271), though the Nature Conservancy Council are at pains to emphasise that this is not a right of way. Nevertheless, it does get you a good way into this forbidden territory without occasioning damage or disturbance to anything. An ascent, due south, from Silverband Shop will take you through the outcrops of Lang Hurst and on to Long Crag, from where another pull will put you at the trig at the eastern end of the long, grassy summit ridge. A simple stroll ensues, high above a vast area of unappetising bogland.
DISTANCE: 12.5 kilometres (7.8 miles)
ASCENT: 485 metres (1590 feet)

2.8c From Hilton There is some suggestion that the aesthetic form of Hilton Beck was carved by an overspill channel from a glacial lake situated around the upper reaches of what is now Maize Beck. Whatever sculpted this splendid defile matters not, it is sufficient that we delight in the handiwork, and walkers wanting a 'legitimate' perambulation without a troubled conscience could do much worse than ascend by Hilton Beck to Maize Beck, and then to make for High Cup Plain, descending from there to Dufton.

There is evidence, too, that before the Warcop Range was developed a miners' track led from Hilton, via Hilton Beck, to the summit of Mickle Fell, making me wonder whether a right of way exists.

Walkers ascending from Hilton may well want to take in Burton Fell en route, from where the target is the western end of the grassy summit ridge, thus avoiding the limestone escarpment along Mickle Fell's southern flank. A more direct line from the top of Hilton Beck may flounder in the bogs along and around Coal Sike, and for this reason is more likely to succeed if you continue along the line of the public footpath to the county boundary and ascend from there, as recommended in Route 2.8a above. Unfortunately, this involves considerable loss of height, all of which has to be regained. Perhaps the bogs (and a pair of wellington boots) are a better option.

In consequence of this multiplicity of options any advice about distances is a rough guess at best, but you should think in terms of some 10 kilometres (6.25 miles), with 555 metres (1820 feet) of ascent, at least.

Route 2.9 Bink Moss Lying in a massive sprawl of wild, heather-clad country Bink Moss (875243) is, for its modest elevation, a challenge for any but the strongest walkers. Many of the paths shown on maps do not exist, and the use of others actively discouraged.

A short distance west of Hargill Bridge a footpath (882214 – signposted) heads north to Hargill Beck, and this may be followed to Hagworm Hill where you should turn east for Bink Moss. The continuation of this path northwards to Forest-in-Teesdale is not so conspicuous as maps would have you believe.

There is no path between the two summits, and the highest point is unmarked, though the remains of a shooting box are to be found nearby.

DISTANCE: 4.7 kilometres (2.9 miles)
ASCENT: 240 metres (790 feet)

This ascent could be used to reach distant Mickle Fell, but requires a day or times when the Warcop Artillery Range are not doing their thing. (See Route 2.7 for further details.)

Route 2.10 Melmerby Fell At an elevation of 580 metres (1900 feet) the summit of Hartside Pass, known as Hartside Cross (646418), is an easy springboard from which to launch an excursion to Melmerby Fell (652380). The top of the pass is a splendid vantage point, and commercial ingenuity has seen to it that there is a cafe and car park nearby, though one gets the impression that these facilities are rather more for the tourist than the walker.

The pass is a former turnpike way, and the most elevated A-road in England until the Stanhope road from Alston (formerly the B6293) was reclassified. Predictably, the pass is often blocked in winter.

The ascent from Alston is fairly gentle by comparison with the twists and turns of the road up from Melmerby, but it is well to remember that walkers venturing from either direction without the support of a car could have long journeys to find shelter should the weather turn bad. Until the road was made, Alston was one of the most isolated towns in England, and many a long and arduous winter must have been experienced there.

The construction of the turnpike road began in 1820, when "the services of the celebrated Mr. MacAdam were put in requisition." Road construction costs nowadays are phenomenal, but it seems things were not much better in the early nineteenth century, "the Commissioners of Greenwich Hospital contributing £30,344 19s 2d towards the cost".

Immediately south of the pass rises Fiends' Fell (the original name of Cross Fell), and also carrying the description 'Gamblesby Allotments'. If you proceed down the road towards Alston for a short way (a large quarried car park on the left, if the cafe car park is crowded) you will find a gate giving access to a track (shown on the 1:50 000 map) running towards Twotop Hill and down eventually to Unthank. Follow this path on beyond a second gate until you can ascend left to the trig on Fiends' Fell. There are no clear pathways here, and the area is seldom visited by walkers, so navigation can be difficult in mist.

Continue south on the highest ground, descending gradually to a marshy col, and then climbing easily first over Little Knapside Hill and then to the summit of Melmerby Fell, marked by a large cairn and a half-hearted stone shelter.

DISTANCE: 4.5 kilometres (2.8 miles)
ASCENT: 130 metres (425 feet)

Walkers wishing to continue to Cross Fell should descend south-east to Meg's Cairn on the Maiden Way, and then follow gradually ascending ground to join the old corpse road between Garrigill and Kirkland beneath Cross Fell screes.

A direct return from Melmerby Fell to Hartside may be avoided by continuing to Meg's Cairn, and then following the Maiden Way north-east to the A686. The Way is confusing to locate from the vicinity of Meg's Cairn if the visibility is not good, due to the presence of a great many distracting cairns. But a compass bearing will put you on the right line, or you can descend due east from the top of Melmerby Fell with a reasonable certainty of recognising the Maiden Way when you reach it. The upper section of the Way as it crosses the shoulders of Melmerby Fell shows sections of the original Roman handiwork, and its line is quite clear. Later the direction becomes less certain, though intermittently cairned, until it reaches a good track from Smittergill Head which you should follow all the way to Rowgill Burn. Cross the burn by a shallow ford, and then ascend to a small copse (shown on the map) before returning to the top of the pass either by following the main road, or by taking the walled track on the south side of the road, rejoining it near an old farm building.

Route 2.11 Round Hill Flanked on the east by the River South Tyne and on the south by the Tees, Round Hill (744361) is a nondescript grassy hill lying in the shadow of Cross Fell. Although lacking significant features Round Hill does adequately meet the bill if you want a short day wandering quietly and undisturbed. Most visitors to Garrigill, it seems, are pursuing or sampling the Pennine Way, and few continue through the village to distant Tyne Head, leaving this corner of the Pennines largely to sheep, birds and a few wild animals.

You can park a car just south of Hill House Farm at 757384, and continue on a good track along the course of the river to Tyne Head, and, if you wish, on across the

Round Hill.

watershed to the Tees. Shortly after starting on the track –
the curious structure on the right with a tree on top of it
was used in the lead-mining days – you reach Dorthgill
Bridge, with the gill itself bubbling down a steep-sided
gully. Cross the bridge and follow the true right (south)
bank of the gill until it eventually peters out high on the
north-eastern shoulder of Round Hill.

A wall runs along the top of Round Hill and so on
leaving the gill behind simply continue ascending until
you meet it. Turn left, following the wall and crossing a
short section of marshy ground containing a small tarn, to
a junction with a fence. A boundary stone projecting from
the base of the wall near this junction is generally thought
to indicate the highest point, but there is slightly higher
ground about 45 metres south-east.

DISTANCE: 2.8 kilometres (1.75 miles)
ASCENT: 235 metres (770 feet)

By descending south-east from the summit you can reach
the watershed on the Tyne Head track, and return to Hill
House in little more than half an hour. Conversely, by
ascending first to Tyne Head, and then to Round Hill
(trackless and heathery) you can continue north along the
wall to Round Hill's subsidiary summit, Noonstones Hill.
A wall descending east will then lead you to within striking
distance of the start.

Route 2.12 Tynehead Fell Walkers intent on a pleasant,
quiet day could do worse than combine Tynehead Fell
(763350) with adjacent Round Hill, the two being easily
served by the old London Lead Mine road that passes
between them. The name describes Tynehead Fell aptly,
though it may not be immediately obvious that its summit
and alternative name, Bellbeaver Rigg, rings of a day
when beavers played the waters of the Tees to the south.

Begin along the broad track that continues beyond the
end of the minor road south of Hill House Farm at 757384.
Numerous cars travel to this roadhead, but few people

bother to venture any further. The track is most pleasant to follow, pursuing the course of the South Tyne. Though no longer immediately obvious there is evidence that the Romans had a camp site along this section of the South Tyne, at a place known as Chesters. Traces of alluvial gravel workings, and the find of some Roman coins, suggest that stretches of the river were worked for lead ore which later research has shown to be far richer in silver than other ores available by deep mining. Walkers wanting to locate Chesters should follow the footpath from Hole House Farm which passes through the camp site, with old shafts and debris lying between the path and the river.

Continue along the mine track until a fence is encountered ascending left on to Tynehead Fell. Follow this on an indistinct path, observing on the way a number of capped mine shafts. The summit lies across a level stretch of marshy ground, and is marked by a cairn.

DISTANCE: 4.5 kilometres (2.8 miles)
ASCENT: 170 metres (555 feet)

There is a second cairn a short distance south, overlooking the Tees and distant Cow Green Reservoir. The views are

The summit of Tynehead Fell (Bellbeaver Rigg), looking to Burnhope Seat.

extensive, with Cross Fell and the Dun Fells seen from an unfamiliar angle, while north-eastwards the range of hills rising to Burnhope Seat marks the boundary between Cumbria and Durham.

Route 2.13 Herdship Fell Herdship Fell (789332) lies almost at the head of Teesdale; a short way north-west, just into Cumbria, the watershed is crossed along the line between Tynehead Fell and Burnhope Seat. The fell is sandwiched between the Tees to the west and Harwood Beck on the east, and is most easily ascended by using the mine road from the car park and picnic area beside the Cow Green Reservoir. This same road, for walkers who wish to avoid the mass of people who use this car park in summer (en route to Cauldron Snout), may be reached from the B6277 (Alston to Middleton road) by a green track leaving the road at 784353.

The walk along the mine road is most pleasant, with distant views of Cross Fell and the two Dun Fells. South-west across the reservoir, Meldon Hill rises in splendid isolation, tempting walkers into a boggy tussle.

Continue to the second group of mine buildings (782328), and follow a vague path ascending the hillside behind them to strike north of east. Soon the path is lost, and though wet in places, the ascent of the fellside is not unduly arduous. The highest point (probably impossible to locate in misty conditions) is marked by a small cairn. Note, however, that this is the second such cairn you will encounter, the first being marginally lower.

DISTANCE: 4.5 kilometres (2.8 miles)
ASCENT: 150 metres (490 feet)

The northern end of Herdship Fell is known as Viewing Hill, with good reason, but this is not a separate summit.

Route 2.14 Thack Moor and Watch Hill from Croglin Known also as Renwick Fell (611463) and Scarrowmanwick Fell these two grassy summits lie west of the main watershed running north from Cross Fell. Infrequently visited, this is an area of solitude and peace involving some strong walking if more than a cursory glance is to be taken.

Along the whole of this western fringe of the Northern Moors runs a series of small, delightful villages – Castle Carrock, Newbiggin, Croglin, Renwick and Melmerby – and days of simple pleasure may be had strolling along their country lanes especially in springtime.

Croglin (575472) stands beside one of the main tributaries of the Eden. A few cars may be parked beside a village hall just on the north side of Croglin Water. From here walk southwards for a short distance until a minor road may be taken to Scarrowmanwick, continuing into the recesses of Croglin valley to a track ascending into a broad gully leading to some old mineworkings. An ascent to the vicinity of the mine (597469) will put you within striking distance of Peel Dod, the northern end of Thack Moor, from where a steep pull will bring you to the trig marking the highest point.

DISTANCE: 5 kilometres (3 miles)
ASCENT: 415 metres (1360 feet)

The continuation to Watch Hill follows a ridge wall, until it changes direction abruptly, after which a direct line for Watch Hill, and the ability to cross an intervening fenceline without occasioning any damage to it, will prove sufficient to take you there in a matter of minutes. Watch Hill is capped by a large cairn at the base of which lies a memorial tablet inscribed 'I. Lowthian Jnr. 1865'.

Walkers returning to Croglin will find the descent via Green Rigg to Renwick and a tramp along the minor roads quite delightful. The continuation to Black Fell involves a certain amount of circumnavigating of walls before a steady pull along the line of a fence/wall brings you to the summit trig.

For really strong walkers, and I mean strong walkers, a walk around the watershed of Croglin Water is not without its attractions. Follow the village road to the cross-roads at 575479 and here turn right on a broad track ascending across the lower slopes of Blotting Raise (not named on the 1:50 000 map) and on to the box at 608495. Continue beyond the box, still on a broad track, until this eventually ends shortly after Croglin Fell. Your objective now is the county boundary (Cumbria–Northumberland) along the broad ridge between Cold Fell to the north, Tom Smith's Stone and Black Fell to the south, but the intervening ground is most difficult, demanding a good deal of patience before reaching the latter summit. Here follow a series of fences and walls along the side ridge north-west to Watch Hill and Thack Moor, before reversing the above route to Scarrowmanwick and Croglin.

DISTANCE: 22.5 kilometres (14 miles)
ASCENT: 560 metres (1835 feet)

Route 2.15 Black Fell from Hartside Cross During the preparation of this book I ascended to Hartside Cross many times, passing from the calm, pastoral landscape of the broad Eden valley into the wild scenery beyond leading onwards to Alston. Wind, snow, rain, and mist I encountered, as well as glorious sunshine, each crossing becoming something to look forward to, for so captivating is the drive up that every ascent was a new experience, enhanced and moulded by the elements. And finally came the days when from the top of the pass I took off into the hills, south to Melmerby Fell (Route 2.10) and Cross Fell, and north over Hartside Height to Black Fell (648444) and Thack Moor.

Begin from a small quarried car park on the Alston side of the pass from the lip of which a fence runs east of north to Hartside Height, your first objective – the going is marginally easier on the west side of the fence, but is nowhere unduly difficult. Benty Hill lies away to your right, and can be reached easily by following the line of another fence running along the connecting ridge.

On Hartside Height the fence gives way to a wall only to

become a fence again a short way further on, setting a pattern that continues all the way to Black Fell (and beyond). Near the summit of Black Fell the wall finally ends, and is succeeded by the inevitable fence leading you to the trig marking the highest point. This final section is a little wet and may necessitate a wide detour, especially after prolonged rain.

DISTANCE: 2.8 kilometres (1.75 miles)
ASCENT: 85 metres (280 feet)

Beyond Black Fell two possibilities face you, both demanding a retracing of one's steps if parked cars have been left at Hartside. But such is the tranquillity and un-spoiled beauty of the rolling hills ahead that to turn about and walk back to Hartside is scarcely a hardship at all.

The first extension to Tom Smith's Stone (and perhaps to Grey Nag) simply follows a fenceline all the way, but demands a fair degree of determination and physical strength to combat the turbulent landscape along the connecting ridge. A second and less demanding extension takes you to distant Thack Moor, crossing the minor summit, Watch Hill, en route. This is a delightful walk, almost entirely dry, and again following either fences or walls. Care needs to be exercised in crossing intermediate walls, which can be avoided but only by lengthy diver-sions.

Route 2.16 Grey Nag Grey Nag (665476) lies roughly west of the village of Alston, at the end of one of the arms stretching out from the main ridge running northwards from Hartside Cross. It may be reached from Hartside, but the round trip is arduous in all but the driest of conditions. An easier ascent may be made from the South Tyne valley, north of Alston, from Castle Nook (696490), following the Pennine Way as it rounds the earthen ram-parts of Whitley Castle, one of many Roman forts which dot the landscape hereabouts.

Once due west of the fort simply strike up the hillside,

across Whitley Common, until the summit ridge wall is reached. The highest point is marked by a cairn and a trig point.

DISTANCE: 3.5 kilometres (2.2 miles)
ASCENT: 365 metres (1200 feet)

Route 2.17 Cold Fell Cold Fell (606556) is the most northerly of the Northern Moors, an isolated and neglected summit, part of the ancient hunting forest of Geltsdale. Its ascent is most easily accomplished from the small group of homes and farm buildings known as Forest Head, in a charming area largely unknown to walkers.

Begin where the minor road through Forest Head takes a sharp bend (583575), at which point an unclear footpath (shown on the 1:50 000 map) heads into an area of disused quarries. Continue through the quarries to gain a broad track circling southwards around Brown Fell, and follow this until a partially collapsed wall appears on the left. Ascend above the wall, following its line, to meet a fence rising sharply up the hillside. Follow the fence which, with but one major change of direction, leads you unerringly to a step stile within a few paces of the large shelter-cairn and trig marking the highest point.

The going can be tedious in wet conditions, but on a fine day is a splendid away-from-it-all alternative to congested routes elsewhere.

DISTANCE: 4.5 kilometres (2.8 miles)
ASCENT: 360 metres (1180 feet)

Route 2.18 Flinty Fell and Nunnery Hill These two minor summits, together with a lower but larger top, Middle Fell, occupy a wedge of moorland south-east of Alston between the South Tyne and Nentdale. Essentially peak-baggers' hills, they hold little attraction, though they do have fine views notably westwards and north-westwards to Cross Fell and the summits around Black Hill. Flinty Fell (771420) also has the distinction of being the most easily ascended 600-metre summit in the whole of the Pennines.

The minor road between Garrigill and Nenthead enables you to approach closely both in height and distance to Flinty Fell, and even closer to Nunnery Hill. From the highest point on the road an easy stroll between gates in adjoining pastures leads to a prominent knoll, the highest point of which is unmarked. Flinty Fell has two summits of equal height 270 metres apart, and this is one of them. The second, across a short stretch of boggy ground, is marked by two large stones and an iron post.

DISTANCE: 0.8 kilometres (0.5 miles)
ASCENT: 20 metres (65 feet)

You can marginally extend this 'ascent' by retracing your steps to the prominent knoll and descending from there to the edge of the conifer plantation nearby to follow a track through the trees to regain the road a short distance west of your starting point. The inclusion of Nunnery Hill, by means of a convenient gate, will only extend your walk by 200 metres, with 12 metres of ascent. The view from Nunnery Hill, however, is better than that from Flinty Fell, but the continuation to Middle Fell too marshy to contemplate.

Route 2.19 The Dodd The Dodd (791458) is one of a number of summits lying along the boundaries of Durham, Northumberland and Cumbria, which collectively afford a series of short, pleasant walks across wide open rolling moorland. The most northerly major hill of this group, The Dodd is embraced by the River Nent to the south and the West Allen to the north, the two rivers almost coming together where the three counties meet on nearby Killhope Moor.

The most obvious line of ascent, curiously starting with a *descent*, is from the highest point of the Nenthead–West Allen Dale road (794444), and follows the line of a fence and later a wall to within striking distance of the summit. The early part of this approach, however, is rather wet, and is best reserved until after prolonged dry weather or a frosty day in winter.

A better, drier ascent begins along the track behind the prominent white farmhouse at Coalcleugh, crossing one of the minor tributaries of the West Allen to a gate, and then pursuing a narrow path upwards through a number of shallow gullies until it joins the route from the top of the road. Here turn right to ascend by a wall to a collapsed stone structure on the edge of the summit plateau, where the wall swings westwards. Continue now roughly east of north, crossing a section of peat groughs to the cairn marking the highest point. A slightly easier line takes the path passing round the summit on its eastern side until it is possible to ascend left to the cairn.

DISTANCE: (From Coalcleugh) 1.7 kilometres (1 mile)
ASCENT: 60 metres (195 feet)

The long descending north ridge of The Dodd is traversed by a number of paths, some better than others, and will be found to be a satisfying alternative ascent/descent by strong walkers with a base in West Allen Dale. Those same walkers will find the tramp along the county boundary across to Whimsey Hill, Hesleywell Moor and Hard Rigg to the track between Clargillhead and Keirsleywell Row an acceptable way of contriving a short circular walk.

Route 2.20 Burtree Fell and Black Hill Gazing northwards down the long valley of East Allen Dale the slight mound of Burtree Fell (862432 – on maps the name is tucked away half way down its southern slopes) is not a summit to occupy much of your time unless you encounter it on a lazy day when musing has a higher priority than marching. The summit lies east of the B6295 road between Allenheads and Weardale, and is easily reached along the county boundary from the highest point on that road (854433). The line is delineated by an alternating sequence, typical in many parts of the Northern Moors, of walls and fences, and the summit reached in a matter of minutes.

DISTANCE: 1 kilometre (0.6 miles)
ASCENT: 32 metres (105 feet)

From the summit you can see the trig point at 868429, a few metres lower, but the intervening ground is marshy. Walkers wishing to continue south to Black Hill will find the going easier along the footpath (shown on the map) running south-east beneath the summit plateau. A descent from there to Cowshill is easy, following the bridleway linking Cowshill and Race Head; a return to the county boundary involves back-tracking.

Route 2.21 Dead Stones and Nag's Head Dead Stones (794399) lies on the boundary between Cumbria and Durham amid high, rolling moorland separating the adjacent valleys of Weardale and Teesdale. The boundary fence is a reliable guide in mist though it will have you in and out of a few bogs, most of which can be avoided.

Begin from Killhope Cross (800433) high on the A689, at 627 metres (2057 feet) the highest A-road in England, where there is room to park a few cars. Follow the boundary over Knoutberry Hill (the going is marginally easier in Cumbria though the path starts off on the Durham side) where it dog-legs on to Nag's Head. A stretch of boggy ground follows (avoidable by a wide detour on the right) leading you to a wall through which there is a gap enabling you to rejoin the fence heading now for Dead Stones.

Medieval crosses on Nag's Head.

The final section to Dead Stones is not difficult, and has fine views to occupy your mind. The summit is marked by a tall, thin cairn on the Durham side of the fence, with a roofed stone shelter nearby looking down over Burnhope Moor to Wearhead and St. John's Chapel.

DISTANCE: 4 kilometres (2.5 miles)
ASCENT: 80 metres (265 feet)

The continuation to Burnhope Seat (the highest summit in this section) is not the easiest walking in the Northern Moors. The line continues to follow the fence, and this will guide you safely all the way, but there are long sections through wet and difficult ground. Perseverance will win in the end.

DISTANCE: 2.5 kilometres (1.6 miles)
ASCENT: 70 metres (230 feet)

Route 2.22 Killhope Law Though far from obvious to the undiscerning eye the hills that form the meeting place of Durham, Northumberland and Cumbria are part of the scene of man's greatest endeavour to win lead from the landscape. Everywhere in these wild, windswept, lonely hills remains abound, in the villages, across the hillsides, high into the numerous radiating dales, or 'hopes' as they are called in this part of the country. Mine shafts dot the maps; tired, sightless ruins of smelt mills, some with chimneys, still fight a losing battle against the elements. But occasionally, as at the Killhope Wheel (826430), modern man (in this case Durham County Council) has stopped long enough to think about this magnificent heritage, and to preserve it for future generations.

Around the head of Weardale swings a great circle of hills reaching, on the northern side of Killhope Burn, their highest point in Killhope Law (819448), all of them to varying degrees affected by this once vast industry, though now the moors echo only to the call of golden plover and grouse.

Killhope Law sits astride the boundary of Durham and

On the summit of Killhope Law.

Northumbria, its summit marked by a trig point, a very tall pole, a drainage ditch, and a massive circular cairn with another pole sprouting from its top. The view is splendid, and the sense of freedom most refined.

The easiest ascent begins along the mine track leaving the minor road between Coalcleugh and East Allen Dale at 814459. Follow this broad track as far as you can, and then strike upwards for the prominent pole on the summit. The terrain is trackless, but the going, through heather and grass, is not unduly arduous, and you soon reach the summit.

DISTANCE: 1.3 kilometres (0.8 miles)
ASCENT: 105 metres (345 feet)

A longer approach may be made along the track from 849465, a short way north of Allenheads, passing a small reservoir, and ascending uneventfully to some shooting cabins just beneath the summit, from where the top is easily reached.

DISTANCE: 3.8 kilometres (2.4 miles)
ASCENT: 295 metres (970 feet)

The continuation south-east along the ridge to Westend Moor is usually dry and leads in due course to the B6295 (Cowshill–Allenheads road) from where the ascent to Killhope Law may also be made.

DISTANCE: 3.8 kilometres (2.4 miles)
ASCENT: 115 metres (380 feet)

Route 2.23 Burnhope Seat and Scaud Hill Visitors to the delightful valley of Weardale may be forgiven if as they drive along they gain the impression there is no escape through the dark, encircling ring of moorland hills that confine the dale beyond Wearhead. The hills, extending in a massive arc around the valley head, form the county boundary between Cumbria and Durham, and rise to their greatest height on Burnhope Seat (788375). All the hills share a combination of grass, heather and peat bog, though nowhere does the latter reach desperate proportions; the col between Burnhope Seat and Scaud Hill does however make a fair attempt at it!

Boggy going notwithstanding a pleasant round can be made over Burnhope Seat and Scaud Hill from the B6277, though it is best left for a clear day. There is room to park

▼ *Killhope Cross, a medieval boundary marker.*

Gunnerside Gill, scene of considerable mining activity. ▼

one or two cars near Darngill Bridge (774371 – not named on the 1:50 000 map), and slightly more space adjoining the county boundary (781358), but the better line is along Darn Gill.

Follow the course of Darn Gill until it bends noticeably north-eastwards, and then continue along a line of shooting butts roughly in the direction of the summit. As you leave the gill behind the way forward is not obvious, so the safest line is to ascend due east until you encounter a fence which runs along the broad summit ridge. This will lead you, one way or another, to the trig pillar (complete with a small flight of steps) marking the highest point in Durham. The highest point of Burnhope Seat, however, lies in Cumbria, due west of the trig, identified by a small cairn, but difficult to locate in poor visibility.

DISTANCE: 1.5 kilometres (0.9 miles)
ASCENT: 165 metres (540 feet)

The continuation to Scaud Hill requires a good sense of direction and a certain amount of perseverance. Follow the boundary fence downwards towards the col between the two hills. Your objective is the right-angled bend the boundary makes at 791369, and it is the knowledge that the boundary fence will guide you both to this junction, or down to the road if necessary, which will help you across the gruesome dose of bog which bedevils the col. In retrospect this stretch of evil ground is far less difficult than it seems, and simply requires a wide detour if you are to continue.

Beyond the sharp bend the maps show another boundary, but all you will find on the ground is a line of tiny stumps to betray the former presence of a fence. They do, however, guide you towards the summit of Scaud Hill, but when they too make a sharp bend (at 794364) you will need a compass bearing to locate the cairn which marks the summit.

DISTANCE: 1.6 kilometres (1 mile)
ASCENT: 14 metres (45 feet)

To return to the B6277 the wisest course is to head due west until you intersect the fenceline along the Durham –Cumbria boundary and follow this downwards.

Route 2.24 Great Stony Hill and Three Pikes Great Stony Hill (824359) is part of the massive sweep of moorland hills which contain Weardale at its head. On the 1:50 000 map its name has slipped northwards down the grassy slopes leading to Burnhope Reservoir, but the rash of stones surrounding the trig on the summit confirms the appropriateness of the name.

There is a path leaving the B6277 near Rough Rigg Farm at 822343 which leads directly to the summit and through a few wet spots. A drier, firmer ascent lies along the broad track starting at 814351 and running past Grass Hill Farm. Follow this track towards Coldberry End, leaving it for the summit across terrain composed mainly of grass with intermittent stony patches, whenever you feel so disposed.

DISTANCE: 1.8 kilometres (1.1 miles)
ASCENT: 145 metres (475 feet)

The track across Coldberry End continues into Weardale, and so a slightly longer ascent may be made from that direction, with the advantage of a short detour to inspect Burnhope Reservoir. Walkers with cars to park are advised not to attempt to proceed beyond the turning in the minor road to the dam of the reservoir; the road ahead becomes narrow, making turning a difficult task. For the walker the way is clear, and as with the approach from Teesdale merely requires a diversion on reaching Coldberry End.

DISTANCE: 3.9 kilometres (2.4 miles)
ASCENT: 275 metres (900 feet)

Strong walkers, prepared to do battle with bog, will find an acceptable circuit from Burnhope Reservoir to Great Stony Hill (easy), Scaud Hill (mucky), Burnhope Seat (arduous), Dead Stones (tolerable), and down over

Lamb's Head to the trig at 821401, returning via the track which gives access to the open moor at 842397. Even with fencelines as a guide for much of the way this is not a circuit to contemplate in poor conditions.

Three Pikes, lying south-east of Great Stony Hill, offers the opportunity of combining two summits in a simple peak-bagging excursion. The broad track to Coldberry End also serves Three Pikes, requiring first a descent from the highest point of the track to pass between the streams which feed Harwood Beck (south) and Ireshope Burn (north) before passing on to the summit.

DISTANCE: 3.5 kilometres (2.2 miles)
ASCENT: 90 metres (295 feet)

Route 2.25 Chapelfell Top and Fendrith Hill Once part of the hunting grounds of the Bishops of Durham, Chapelfell Top (876346) is a better mountain to look at than to walk upon. Its neighbour, Fendrith Hill, fares somewhat better. Both summits are best seen from the Newbiggin–Westgate road as it crosses Westernhope Moor, and the views from the ridge along which they lie are high, wide and handsome. These modest heights with easy motorable access are predictably popular with skiers, and a frozen state of affairs underfoot may well be the most propitious time to tackle them.

At the top of the Langdon Beck–St. John's road (863350) there is room to park a few cars from which to launch an attack on Chapelfell Top. There is no path, and if there was it would probably be consumed by the shifting morass that lies ahead. Make your ascent on a clear day and in a spirit of optimism and thou shalt be rewarded.

DISTANCE: 1.5 kilometres (0.9 miles)
ASCENT: 90 metres (295 feet)

The continuation to Fendrith Hill lies almost due south and the going improves the further you distance yourself

In the upper reaches of Gunnerside Gill.

from Chapelfell Top. The summit is marked by a trig point.

DISTANCE: 1.3 kilometres (0.8 miles)
ASCENT: 11 metres (35 feet)

The ascent to Fendrith Hill from the Newbiggin–Westgate road (Swinhope Head) is much less aggravated by difficult terrain, though there is a stretch of bog shortly after Dora's Seat, in close proximity to the ski tow. The line follows alternating walls and fences en route gently to the summit.

DISTANCE: 2.2 kilometres (1.4 miles)
ASCENT: 90 metres (295 feet)

Walkers who enjoy solitude and tracing neglected foot-paths might find the path from Ettersgill to Swinhope

Head an interesting approach. A return from Fendrith Hill to the track on Church Bowers and down again to Ettersgill completes a modest circuit.

DISTANCE: 10 kilometres (6.25 miles)
ASCENT: 315 metres (1035 feet)

Route 2.26 Outberry Plain Outberry Plain (923326) is a high moorland summit sandwiched between Teesdale and Weardale; it has no special merit, but is a useful alternative during summer to congested routes elsewhere.

The simplest ascent begins from Swinhope Head at the highest point of the Newbiggin–Westgate road, where there is room to park a few cars. Begin by heading east on a broad track following the line of a wall and later a fence to a gate. Pass through the gate and continue with the fence across trackless and occasionally wet ground all the way to the summit trig, which is set amid rapidly deteriorating terrain.

DISTANCE: 2.7 kilometres (1.7 miles)
ASCENT: 70 metres (230 feet)

The continuation to Harnisha Hill or to Carrs Hill is largely bedevilled by difficult going, and though an extension of this walk is possible to Carrs Hill in particular with an easy descent to the mineworkings near Marl and Hudeshope Becks, it is not advisable in other than the driest conditions. An old track links Hudeshope with Moor House on the Newbiggin road, and there is a way through Hardberry Gutter, both of which provide interest and a longer walk.

Section 3 – The Howgill Fells

	MAP REFERENCE	HEIGHT (m)	1:50 000 OS MAP
The Calf	667971	676	98
Calders (Brant Fell)	671960	674	98
Bram Rigg Top	668965	672	98

Great Dummacks	679963	663	98
White Fell Head	661974	646	97/98
Fell Head	649982	640	97
Yarlside	686985	639	98
Randygill Top	687001	625	91
Bush Howe	659981	623	97/98
Arant Haw	662946	605	98
Green Bell	699011	605	91
Simon's Seat	660999	587	91/97/98
Hooksey	685009	586	91
Hazelgill Knott	673997	578	98
Kensgriff	688993	574	98
Stockless	694006	568	91
West Fell	670015	542	91
Uldale Head	641000	530	91/97
Blease Fell	624004	474	91
Winder	654933	473	97

ROUTES

3.1 The Calf from Sedbergh
3.2 The Calf from Castley and Birkhaw
3.3 Fell Head and The Calf from Fairmile Gate
3.4 Uldale Head and Blease Fell
3.5 Simon's Seat via Langdale
3.6 The Calf, Calders and Great Dummacks via Cautley Spout
3.7 The Calf from Brow Foot over West Fell and Hazelgill Knott
3.8 Randygill Top from Brow Foot over Hooksey
3.9 Yarlside and Randygill Top from Cautley
3.10 Green Bell and Randygill Top from Weasdale
3.11 The Fairmile Circuit

Were it not for the M6 motorway barging through the Lune Gorge, the Howgill Fells would be largely unknown to the hill-walking fraternity, set aside as they are from the main line of the Pennine Mountains, and not quite having a foot in the Lake District. As it is they are still relatively little known, and form a unique, untramped wilderness of remarkable charm and beauty; the walker in search of solitude will be well pleased with the Howgills. In *The Old Hand-Knitters of the Dales* (1951) by Marie Hartley and Joan Ingilby we find the Howgills described as "hump-backed hills as sleak as seal skin, [that] reflect the sunlight like shot-silk".

Encompassed (perhaps entriangled would be a better word) by the Lune Gorge on the west, the headwaters of the Lune flowing through Ravenstonedale to the north, and the Rathey valley to the east, the Howgills are a splendid cluster of steep-sided, bald-domed fells, standing in an area of outstanding and simple beauty. Sir Clement Jones comments: "Wherever you look in the Howgills everything is composed and in the right spot and there is nothing to jar." They are of slate, not the ubiquitous limestone that predominates in the Pennines, and their geological affinity is with the Lake District and the low fells around Windermere. Bearing more than a passing resemblance to the superb northern ridges of the Brecon Beacons in South Wales, many of the Howgill ridges offer excellent long walks on velvety turf, unrestricted by walls, fences and enclosures. This is free range country, the fells rising abruptly from glaciated valleys, their sides folded into deep, shadowy gullies, and their lines unbroken, except at Cautley and in the recesses of Carlin Gill, by outcrops of rock. It is a region of haunting attraction, inhabited by black-faced Rough Fell sheep, that regard you with mild surprise, long-haired wild fell ponies ranging freely across the tops, and buzzard, kestrel, curlew and snipe.

Unhappily, their very featurelessness is a real danger in poor visibility, and with the prospect of help far away, clear days and companions are highly recommended. Here, far above the humdrum world of every day, patience is truly rewarded, for there is no finer view than that which awaits the visitor to the lonely trig point on The Calf, nor anywhere a more pervading air of relaxation.

At a more prosaic level, full enjoyment of the Howgills is impeded by the lack of convenient coverage on maps.

The clinical conformity that otherwise endears you to the Ordnance Survey 1:50 000 map has here carved the fells on to portions of three separate sheets (91, 97 and 98), and though partly within the Yorkshire Dales National Park, they lie just outside the scope of the excellent 1:25 000 Outdoor Leisure Maps of the Dales. For use on the Karrimor International Two-day Mountain Marathon, Harvey Map Services have produced a single sheet at 1:40 000 covering all the fells and the adjoining Wild Boar Fell and Baugh Fell, and walkers who can operate at this scale will find this edition of considerable help. For my money, however, the temporary lack of an Outdoor Leisure Map, which hopefully the Ordnance Survey will produce in the not too distant future, can best be alleviated by obtaining the two OS 1:25 000 Pathfinder Series (Sheets NY 60/70 and SD 69/79), which, apart from the frilly colours illuminating the OLMs, are otherwise more or less identical. For the purposes of the routes which ensue I have assumed that walkers have adopted my advice and procured the two maps in question.

Route 3.1 The Calf from Sedbergh Pronounced 'Sedber', Sedbergh reposes splendidly against a backcloth of the high, green, rounded domes of the Howgill Fells,

On the summit of The Calf.

enjoying a relationship that few other towns in England can boast. It is a quiet, unassuming market town, possessing a long-established public school, and is an excellent centre for a walking holiday – though the overriding impression is that this charming community isn't quite up to mass tourism. Unlike much of the Howgills, Sedbergh is caught within the bureaucratic boundary of the Yorkshire Dales National Park, and sports a National Park Information Centre in a converted eighteenth-century shop where George Bernard Shaw used to purchase his socks.

Dominated (if that isn't too harsh a word for these gentle giants) by a satellite of the Howgills, Winder (pronounced with a short 'i', as in the meteorological wind), Sedbergh proves a useful access point for these fells, the highest of which is far out of sight, but attainable by the most pleasant of routes.

Start from the car park (658919) near the church and walk towards the centre of the town, turning left and almost immediately right to follow the road signposted to Howgill – a very small hamlet some distance away which has contrived to lend its name to the whole range of fells.

Follow this minor road until at 652923 you can take a track, right (signposted 'To the Fell'), leading to Lockbank Farm. Incline right through the farm buildings, and pass through two iron gates to reach the open fellside. Here turn left and climb an initially steep green path slanting across the lower slopes of Winder. There is an immediate and delightful opening-up of the panorama southwards stretching from Morecambe Bay to distant Whernside and the central Pennines, though the gradient, for a while, has a tendency to sort out the weak from the knackered!

As the ground levels, bear right to pass around the side of Winder (keeping the fell on your left), and continue on a good path, through delightful, simply constructed scenery and across a splendid, narrow (but easy) saddle all the way to Calders (also known as Brant Fell).

Ascending to The Calf.

Calders and Bram Rigg Top.

Two diversions from this route are possible, and recommended (though not measured). The first takes in Winder itself, attainable from the stretch of level ground either by a direct, narrow path which shoots up the fellside, or by curving left and then following the broad west ridge – this

Arant Haw from Calders.

is the better. The second diversion allows you to take in Arant Haw by a new and direct path not shown on maps, leaving the main path due south of the summit and making a beeline for it. If you are obliged to return this way, then it makes sense to accommodate both these summits in one direction, at least.

From the large cairn on the summit of Calders the way ahead, indistinct for a few metres, leads by a good path across the shoulder of Bram Rigg Top to an easy pull to the summit of The Calf.

DISTANCE: 6.8 kilometres (4.25 miles) (from the car park)
ASCENT: 575 metres (1885 feet)

Walkers who do not wish to return to Sedbergh by the same route will find Route 3.2 in reverse (especially the route to Birkhaw), followed by a not unduly long return along the Roman road (Howgill Lane), a pleasant conclusion to the day.

Route 3.2 The Calf from Castley and Birkhaw Castley (not to be confused with Cautley, 6 kilometres to the east) and Birkhaw are both active farms on the extreme western fringe of the Howgills, lying a short distance and accessible from the Roman road (Howgill Lane) that runs from Sedbergh to Tebay. Farm tracks, in some places deeply rutted, facilitate easy access to the fells, and by combining both routes described here, a rewarding and not too difficult circuit may be constructed. The one major problem is the paucity of parking opportunity along Howgill Lane, on which I can offer little suggestion save that of walking from beyond the intake wall at Fairmile Gate, or down towards Lowgill and the Crook of Lune Bridge.

3.2a From Castley Castley Farm is gained from Howgill Lane at Four Lane Ends (632959), and a good, wide track followed past the farm buildings to gain the open fell at a gate in the intake wall (641959). From here descend north-eastwards to cross Long Rigg Beck, later to become Chapel Beck (sometimes awkward after prolonged rain), and gain the obvious path ascending roughly eastwards to the top of White Fell Head. Near the confluence of Long Rigg Beck and Calf Beck is a group of small circles of stones thought to be the remains of the hut dwellings of the early settlers in this region.

There is no doubt that here you are truly among the fells; fine curving shapes soar all around, the gills and

Randygill Top and Kensgriff.

becks gurgle, the moorland sighs, and the spirit rises perceptibly. And as you ascend to White Fell Head there is a good view of the 'Horse of Busha' (or Bush Howe), a uniquely formed patch of dark rocks fallen naturally into the rough shape of a horse.

From the top of White Fell Head, the actual summit (unmarked) being passed by the path, the continuation to the trig on The Calf is easily attainable.

DISTANCE: 4 kilometres (2.5 miles) (from Four Lane Ends)

ASCENT: 495 metres (1625 feet)

3.2b From Birkhaw The track to Birkhaw leaves Howgill Lane at 636945, and continues through a series of gates and by a delightful walk to the intake wall at 642948. Here turn left and follow a rutted farm track to a sheepfold near the confluence of Bram Rigg Beck and Swarth Greaves Beck (650957). Cross the stream and ascend to gain the ridge to Bram Rigg Top near some interesting rock cuttings. Approaching the summit the path inclines left, missing out the summit of Bram Rigg, though for no valid reason except the saving of a paltry few calories of energy; purists and connoisseurs will find the summit marked by one or two stones, sufficiently few to be moved about as

Randygill Top, Kensgriff and Yarlside.

walkers disagree over exactly which is the highest spot. But who cares? Bram Rigg's grassy summit is invariably ignored by the masses, and the view westwards is quite supreme.

The continuation to The Calf is an uncomplicated affair, making for the conspicuous path between it and Calders.

DISTANCE: 5 kilometres (3.1 miles)
ASCENT: 530 metres (1740 feet)

As suggested earlier, combining both these routes will give an excellent and rewarding excursion into these fells from the west.

Route 3.3 Fell Head and The Calf from Fairmile Gate One of the longest routes to The Calf (667971), the ascent over Linghaw and Fell Head (649982) more than amply compensates by providing a delightfully simple ridge walk that most walkers will find pleasing. Used as the first half of the Fairmile Circuit (Route 3.11), the route is an excellent introduction to the Howgills.

The minor road which follows the line of the Roman road through the Lune valley is exceedingly narrow, and affords no opportunity to park cars; the open pastureland beyond Fairmile Gate, where the road is no longer contained by walls, by contrast offers plenty of space.

Fell Head may be reached from Beck Houses (634967) by the footpath shown on the 1:50 000 and 1:25 000 maps, one of the few public footpaths in the Howgills, but a better (and tougher) start may be made by first tackling Linghaw. Follow the obvious grassy path which roughly and steeply follows the line of Dry Gill until, as the gradient eases, you can move right to gain this minor summit (its highest point marked by a small collection of stones), with Fell Head comprising much of the high ground to the south-east. Linghaw is an excellent vantage point for the Lune valley, the low eastern fells of Lakeland beyond the motorway, and the Kent Estuary.

Continue south-eastwards on a faint path descending to the col crossed by the path coming up from Beck Houses. Cross the col and ascend again to Fell Head's subsidiary summit (marked by a small, untidy cairn), and then climb easily to the main summit, identified by a large cairn with a pole sticking from it. The route now curves around the top of Long Rigg Beck to descend steeply to a neat col, Windscarth Wyke, and from there ascends steadily to the minor top, Bush Howe, where a good path, descending slightly at first, makes for the distant, prominent trig point on The Calf.

DISTANCE: 5.3 kilometres (3.3 miles)
ASCENT: 595 metres (1950 feet)

The continuation to Calders is described in Route 3.6.

Route 3.4 Uldale Head and Blease Fell Walkers whose philosophy restricts them to summits exceeding 600 metres, 2000 feet or some similar silly constraint will give neither of these grassy tops so much as a passing glance. The loss is theirs, for mere altitude is an eminence of undeserved merit no better illustrated than among these unassuming fringe summits of the Howgills.

The delightful Langdale valley hemmed in by the snow-dusted Howgill fells.

The delightful prospect of spring snow on the northern Howgill fells.

There is a short, speedy ascent of Blease Fell (624004) through the gate adjoining the small copse at 617003, climbing diagonally across the sloping meadow to another gate in the intake wall, from where you curve gradually around the shoulder of the fell on a grassy path until it disappears in wet ground above Grains Gill, leaving you to pick your way easily through a few peat hags to gain a summit marked only by a few stones. But this is fare for no more than a short half day. Each of the two following routes however, both fine circuits, is a vastly different proposition, and will appeal greatly to anyone who enjoys long, lonely walks.

3.4a Via Ellergill Start near the telephone box (641054) at Gaisgill, and take the farm track to Ellergill, passing through two gates to gain a track beyond the farm buildings, and continue southwards for 2.5 kilometres (1.6 miles) until the wall on your left descends towards Langdale. Here simply follow the rising ground to Rispa Pike and on to Uldale Head (641000), the summit of which is unmarked.

Winter in the Howgills.

Approaching the summit of The Calf along the West Fell/Hazelgill Knott ridge.

The continuation to Blease Fell crosses untracked ground to the damp col of Archer Moss, from where the summit is easily attained.

Hare Shaw is more prominent from the top of Blease Fell than the long ridge to Tebay, and will afford an easy return to Gaisgill. Somewhat better, in my view, however,

Descending the Hazelgill Knott/West Fell ridge.

is the companion ridge over Powson Knott and Roger Howe to come down to Tebay near Mount Pleasant, from where a pleasant 2 kilometres (1.25 miles) along the minor road will take you back to Gaisgill.

DISTANCE: 12 kilometres (7.5 miles)
ASCENT: 385 metres (1265 feet)

3.4b Via Carlin Gill This is no place to take your granny in a bath chair, nor to venture if you are unhappy on awkward terrain or friable ground. But the blithe spirit will find this concealed nook the most absorbing gem the Howgills has to offer, a route that sparkles all the more for its unsuspected presence, though passing motorists may well have wondered what lay within the overlapping folds of fellside that gathered to the east of the motorway. Like Langdale further east, the valley of Carlin Gill wends an innocuous way into the heart of the fells in a most endearing fashion, pulling you on to discover what lies beyond. And what you find is quite magical.

Begin at Carlingill Bridge (624996), on the very edge of the Yorkshire Dales National Park – a boundary which coincides with that between Cumbria and North Yorkshire. Continue along the north (true right) bank of the gill until Weasel Gill comes in from your left, and here cross Carlingill Beck to gain a well-trodden sheep track on the opposite bank, taking you into a most pleasant sanctum that for some time has you wondering what all the fuss is about.

And then you find out! The valley, a firm favourite with dippers and grey wagtails, suddenly, dramatically narrows, forcing you to recross the gill and at times to grapple with collapsed and recumbent trees, and boulders that in times of spate are well and truly submerged (barring further progress). A broad gash begins to open up on the right, and a short way further on you find yourself at the foot of the enormous chasm of Black Force down which spill a number of small waterfalls. But more lies beyond, for, after sparring a few rounds with the beck, along which incidentally lies a superb water slide spilling into a small, deep pool of crystal water, you arrive at the foot of a splendid waterfall, The Spout, very efficiently halting forward progress. There are two escapes: one very steeply up the shaly and later grassy fellside behind you, to gain a horizontal path; the other by a narrow rib containing the waterfall in a small amphitheatre. A staircase of footsteps takes you steeply upwards only to face you with a pre-

Carlingill Bridge: the ascent into Carlin Gill starts here.

carious few moments on friable rock before the security of firm ground above the waterfall. Continue from here simply by following the beck as closely as conditions allow, the nearer the better.

Finally, both escapes merge on the edge of a broad grassy plateau, Blakethwaite Bottom, from where Uldale Head is gained by a steepish pull up grassy slopes.

Such an inspiring ascent deserves a better return than the mere grassy descents apparently on offer. For this reason I recommend a start, not at Carlingill Bridge, but at Salterwath Bridge (612009), which allows you to stretch your legs before reaching Carlingill Bridge, and permits a descent from Blease Fell, along its fine north ridge until you can drop left to a disused quarry near Lune's Bridge (614030), and return to Salterwath Bridge via Brockholes, along the banks of the River Lune. Keep ahead on entering the farm yard, turning right immediately after the buildings to reach the river and follow the edge of the meadow, lush in spring with wild flowers – speedwell, meadow cranesbill, clover, herb robert and wild garlic. A path finally leads you through a short stretch of woodland, back to the bridge.

DISTANCE: 12 kilometres (7.5 miles)
ASCENT: 450 metres (1475 feet)

The start of the walk into Carlin Gill.

The upper reaches of Carlin Gill.

Near the top of Carlin Gill.

Route 3.5 Simon's Seat via Langdale One of the most endearing features about the Howgill Fells is the consummate ease with which you can construct day-long walks that combine fine, airy ridges and deeply gouged, delightful valleys. The long approaches from the north exemplify this, offering both high- and low-level walks, and the following visit to neglected Simon's Seat (660999) is a typical example.

Start from the village of Longdale (not, curiously, Langdale – though signposts, writers and cartographers all dispute the proper name), where parking may be found near the old school, and continue ahead along the minor road for a hundred metres until, as you approach the gate giving access to Town Head Farm, another gate appears on the left. Go left here and follow a broad, walled track imaginatively named Cowbound Lane. The wall on your right takes a divergent line after a short while, but continue ahead on a rutted track until another wall appears on the right, leading you finally to a gate giving access to the open fellside.

Turn right here, on a good, broad track which later starts to descend towards Langdale Beck. Just before the start of the descent a track opts to pursue the high ground, and if followed will take you to Langdale Knott and ultimately on to West Fell to join Route 3.7 from Brow Foot to The Calf. For Simon's Seat, however, drop down to Langdale Beck by a slanting path heading into the valley. Langdale is a most beautiful valley, and tracks run on both sides of the beck, but that on the south side (reached by boulder-hopping across the beck near the bottom of the slanting path) will lead you to a triple sheepfold, at the confluence between Langdale Beck and Nevy Gill. Cross the gill near the sheepfold and ascend the steep grassy fellside beyond, not a difficult undertaking, but plagued by numerous false summits before the cairn on Simon's Seat is reached.

DISTANCE: 6 kilometres (3.75 miles)
ASCENT: 385 metres (1265 feet)

The view towards The Calf from Simon's Seat, especially if you move slightly off the summit and ensconce yourself among the tussock grass for lunch, is quite delightful, while at your feet Langdale soldiers on, splitting into East and West Grain and at its highest point draining the waters of The Calf itself. To the west the Lakeland fells range themselves impressively across the horizon, while the high Pennines, Cross Fell, the Dun Fells and Mickle Fell, stretch away to the north. Eastwards, peering between minor bumps along the West Fell–Hazelgill Knott ridge, rise Wild Boar Fell and Swarth Fell, their long low profiles belying the pleasurable walking to be had across their tops.

Route 3.6 The Calf, Calders and Great Dummacks from Cautley Cautley Spout, a series of splendid and dramatic cascades, falls only a short distance east of The Calf (667971), and an ascent to the highest of the Howgill Fells by this route is a rewarding experience. As is the case with many of the Howgills, this approach may be extended to form a complete circuit, thus avoiding the necessity of retracing one's outward route.

Start near the Cross Keys Temperance Hotel at 698969, near which there is room to park a few cars, and, in an excellent footbridge, the means of crossing the River Rawthey. The hotel is now a National Trust property, and described as "A small whitewashed inn, built circa 1600 and altered in the early eighteenth and late nineteenth centuries. Acquired in 1949 with 17 acres of land, under the Will of Mrs. E. A. Bunney, to be held as an unlicensed inn in memory of her sister Miss M. B. Hewetson." Unlicensed it may be, but modern philosophy has a curious way of solving minor inconveniences of this nature – simply take your own booze, providing you are having a meal. 'Temperance', however, does still extend to the prohibition on smoking.

Once across the river, bear left on a clear and sometimes damp path entering a pleasant flat-bottomed valley and making for the distant white splash of Cautley Spout at the right-hand edge of the broken cliffs of Cautley Crag – imposing, but of no interest to the rock climber. As you near the falls two possibilities emerge: one, to ascend by a faint path climbing beside the falls, the other to stay with a better path making for Bowderdale Head where an offshoot curls back above the spout and later climbs to join the main track descending from The Calf to Bowderdale.

As the gradient eases a small unnamed tarn is encountered (671975) at the head of the West Fell–Hazelgill Knott route from Brow Foot (Route 3.7). Of the two routes which then shortly appear the more obvious curves away from The Calf, continuing along the broad ridge to Bush Howe, while the left fork takes you directly to the summit trig.

DISTANCE: 4 kilometres (2.5 miles)
ASCENT: 495 metres (1625 feet)

The continuation to Calders follows a broad path across the eastern shoulder of Bram Rigg Top before an easy pull to the large cairn on the summit.

DISTANCE: 1.1 kilometres (0.7 miles)
ASCENT: 40 metres (130 feet)

The Spout: Carlin Gill.

Great Dummacks (which sounds like an apt way of describing a few people I know) is reached by initially following a fenceline eastwards, and when it turns to disappear along Middle Tongue continue ahead on to a tussocky plateau, the highest point of which, to all except the Ordnance Survey, is a little in doubt.
DISTANCE: 0.9 kilometres (0.6 miles)
ASCENT: 12 metres (40 feet)

There is no immediately obvious way off Great Dummacks, and for this reason none should be attempted in poor visibility. The easiest tack is to move south-eastwards, around the southern edge of Cautley Crag, and to descend alongside Pickering Gill to Cautley Holme Beck and the outward route. By completing the circuit in this way you will have travelled 8.2 kilometres (5.1 miles) and ascended through 550 metres (1800 feet).

Route 3.7 The Calf from Brow Foot over West Fell and Hazelgill Knott The long northern ridges of the Howgills, and their attendant river-bottomed valleys, are delightful walking country, enabling appetising traverses or extended circular walks to be composed almost at will. The ease of the going underfoot, mostly short, velvety turf, the absence of rock outcrops, and the sparsity of walls and fences all contrive to imbue the visitor with a refined sense of contentment, solitude and tranquillity, something you will be hard pressed to experience to quite the same degree elsewhere in the Pennines.

Only as an ultimate objective is The Calf (667971) included in this walk, you can just as easily omit it and detract little, except its superb panorama, from the walk, especially if you elect to return to Brow Foot along the course of Bowderdale Beck.

Brow Foot lies just south of the A685 at 683049, and beyond it, a short way along the left fork you encounter, it is possible to park a car on open pastureland without hindering farm vehicles. The right fork leads to a small group of farm buildings, Bowderdale (signposted from the A685). Cross Bowderdale Bridge and ascend a short distance until you can leave the road, left, immediately before a cattle grid, to follow a rutted farm track made by tractors alongside a wall. Continue on this track to and beyond the intake wall.

By paralleling the line of the intake wall you come shortly to the entrance to the long valley of Bowderdale, not at all unlike many Scottish glens, especially when mist shrouds the tops. Where the path dips to enter Bowderdale (669035) simply continue ahead, climbing easily as you gain the slopes of West Fell. The farm track, faint in places and evidence of how easily these fells may be travelled, now pursues a southwards course, and takes you by a series of minor hillocks and twists and turns finally to Hazelgill Knott and to the very lip of The Calf plateau, before crossing easily to the summit trig.

DISTANCE: 9.3 kilometres (5.8 miles)
ASCENT: 435 metres (1430 feet)

The trek through Bowderdale is a superb walk in its own right, descending near Cautley Spout to gain a series of paths that will eventually lead you to Sedbergh. Or, by following the path climbing out of Bowderdale to The Calf, joining the ridge route near a small tarn, you can continue over Calders and Winder to reach Sedbergh by a combination low- and high-level route.

Strong walkers returning to Brow Foot should consider tackling Yarlside, Kensgriff and Randygill Top, before returning by way of Green Bell (route 3.10 in reverse). This would give a circular walk of some 21 kilometres (13 miles) and involve 925 metres (3035 feet) of ascent.

Route 3.8 Randygill Top from Brow Foot over Hooksey Start as for Route 3.7 from the open pastureland near Brow Foot, but instead of heading for Bowderdale, walk south on a minor track which, at the turning (682042) to Scar Sikes Farm, deteriorates to a tractor track eventually leading you on to the open fellside. Follow this track, at times indistinct, to a curious angle of low stone wall, from where it is an easy pull to the elongated north–south ridge of Hooksey on which the track reappears, to be followed uneventfully to the unmarked summit of this northerly outlier.

The continuation to Randygill Top (687001) is by Leathgill Bridge, but a bridge only in the sense of a narrow col joining the two mountains and diverting the fell waters west into Leath Gill (a good escape, back to Bowderdale, in the event of a change in the weather) and east into Weasdale Beck. The col may be difficult to locate in mist, but represents the way forward to gain the foot of the northern slopes of Randygill Top which are steep, but mercifully short, and will place you close by the large cairn on the summit.

DISTANCE: 5.5 kilometres (3.4 miles)
ASCENT: 455 metres (1490 feet)

The continuation to Green Bell, on whose eastern slopes rise the waters of the River Lune, follows a narrow path north-eastwards to the minor summit, Stockless, on which a better track is encountered. This in turn passes through the gap between Green Bell and its south-west summit, but from which an obvious walkers' path romps up to the summit trig.

DISTANCE: 1.5 kilometres (0.9 miles)
ASCENT: 65 metres (215 feet)

Route 3.9 Yarlside and Randygill Top from Cautley
From the footbridge (698969) across the River Rawthey at Cautley a straightforward ascent may be made of Yarlside (686985) by tackling the fellside head on, always pursuing the easiest gradient until the elongated summit is reached. But this is neither interesting nor especially rewarding except for the glimpses into the secluded valley of Westerdale it affords. The simple fact of the matter is that the main attraction hereabouts is Cautley Spout, and any ascent which misses the opportunity of visiting this splendid fall doesn't want for lack of imagination!

Route 3.6 describes the approach to Cautley Spout, and time should be allowed to divert for a close inspection. Back on route, continue by a prominent, broad path to the high col, Bowderdale Head, and ascend obliquely, right, into the wide ravine from which springs Bowderdale Beck. Easier going is found on the south (true left) bank of the beck, but in winter both flanks provide ample opportunity for crampon and ice-axe practice – with due care, of course! Yarlside has two summits, though the southernmost scarcely raises itself above the general lie of the land. It is the northern summit, marked by a large cairn, which is the higher point.

DISTANCE: 3 kilometres (1.9 miles)
ASCENT: 460 metres (1510 feet)

A shortened circuit may be made by descending Yarlside's north-west ridge, a broad, grassy affair, leading you into the heart of Bowderdale at the confluence of Randy Gill and Bowderdale Beck, from where a return may be made to Bowderdale Head – but take care not to stray too far along the prominent path on the west side of the beck before crossing it, as the valley opens out a little: the main path will have you clambering up to The Calf if you are not careful!

The continuation to Kensgriff and Randygill Top involves a very steep, grassy descent to the Saddle, requiring good compass work in mist, and proving hazardous in icy conditions. Kensgriff itself is of little importance, but its narrow, ridge-like form leads you easily to the foot of Randygill Top, the ascent of which is made by means of a narrow footpath, until this peters out, followed by easy grass-work to reach the cairned summit.

DISTANCE: 2 kilometres (1.25 miles)
ASCENT: 200 metres (655 feet)

A descent of Randygill Top's south-west shoulder will take you into Bowderdale to effect the return described above. Better, and requiring little description, is an extension over Stockless and Grere Fell eastwards to take in Harter Fell, followed by a descent to Murthwaite Farm, regaining the A683 at Handley's Bridge (706976).

Route 3.10 Green Bell and Randygill Top from Weasdale

Weasdale is a community of scattered farms and cottages south-west of Newbiggin-on-Lune, with extensive tree nurseries. It is an isolated spot, with a settled air about it that makes it a relaxing starting point for a trip into the fells.

Start along the cart track which leaves the minor road at 694039 (though the track from 702042 serves just as well). Follow the track as it climbs first beside a wall and later turns to pass between two small knolls, Low and High Knott, between which Will Gill, a side stream of Weasdale Beck, flows from a stretch of marshy ground higher up. Leave the track, such as it is now, and cross the wet ground to gain the second track (from 702042) just below the shoulder known as Stwarth. This should now be followed to the col between Green Bell (699011) and its south-west summit, with the higher point being easily attainable by a more direct line anywhere in the last half kilometre. The summit, marked by a trig point, is a delightful dome of grass, and a few insignificant springs a mere 300 metres north-east of the summit prove to be the birthplace of the River Lune, and as such worth a visit, though there is no evidence that anyone ever does.

DISTANCE: 3 kilometres (1.9 miles)
ASCENT: 320 metres (1050 feet)

The continuation to Randygill Top follows a good path from the trig, south-west across the minor top, Stockless, to a col at the head of Weasdale Beck. A prominent path goes left here, contouring across the slopes of Randygill Top, but a narrow path ascends from the col to the large cairn on the summit.

DISTANCE: 1.7 kilometres (1 mile)
ASCENT: 85 metres (275 feet)

A steep descent northwards to cross Leathgill Bridge, a fine saddle in a depression along the Randygill Top–Hooksey ridge, facilitates an excellent round trip with only a few minor navigational problems at the end in order to get back to Weasdale – and these can be easily resolved by using the 1:25 000 OS Sheet NY 60/70.

Route 3.11 The Fairmile Circuit This concoction is an unashamed attempt to obtain maximum pleasure from a western approach to the Howgills at one go; it is a delightful introduction to the fells in general.

Start as described in Route 3.3 for Fell Head (including the stiff pull to Linghaw first), and continue to The Calf. From The Calf a broad path presses on east of south, making for Calders, and en route bypassing Bram Rigg Top, a minor summit topped by two or three stones which render service as a cairn; walkers wanting to visit Bram Rigg Top should divert from the main path, which otherwise ignores this outlier.

It is an easy, though largely pointless, exercise to digress from Calders to visit Great Dummacks, the highest point of which is at 679963, though only walkers with surveying aptitude could be sure of finding it on the ground! But, if it's a nice day, wander out and back, by all means, a good path following a fenceline starting you off in the right direction, but shortly leaving you to work out your own salvation.

From Calders parallel the fenceline south-west and then south on a broad track as it descends steeply to a narrow col. This track ultimately continues to Winder and Sedbergh, but leave it behind just after the col and aim for the top of Arant Haw (marked by a collapsed cairn), and from there descend the long western ridge to reach the confluence of Bram Rigg Beck and Chapel Beck beneath the minor hump of Castley Knotts. If the becks are in spate, crossing can be a problem, but your objective from here is to follow the intake wall, initially upwards as you round Castley Knotts, all the way back to Fairmile. The going is nowhere difficult, and provides a fitting conclusion to a pleasant round trip.

DISTANCE: 13.5 kilometres (8.4 miles)
ASCENT: 805 metres (2640 feet)

Section 4 The Dales

	MAP REFERENCE	HEIGHT (m)	1:50 000 OS MAP
The Three Peaks			
Whernside	739816	736	98
Ingleborough	741746	723	98
Pen y Ghent	838734	694	98
Plover Hill	849752	680c	98
Simon Fell	755752	650	98
Park Fell	764770	563	98
Blea Moor	773826	535	98
Wensleydale and Widdale			
Great Shunner Fell	849973	716	98
Lovely Seat	879951	675	98
Great Knoutberry Hill (Widdale Fell)	789872	672	98
Dodd Fell Hill	841846	668	98
Drumaldrace (Wether Fell)	874867	614	98
Mallerstang, Garsdale and Dentdale			
High Seat (Mallerstang Edge)	802012	709	91/92
Wild Boar Fell	758988 760988 761985	708	98
Hugh Seat	809991	689	98
Great Coum	701836	687	98
Swarth Fell	756967	681	98
Baugh Fell (Tarn Rigg Hill)	741916	678	98
Baugh Fell (Knoutberry Haw)	731919	676	98

Lunds Fell	809971	667	98
Nine Standards Rigg	825061	662	91/92
Swarth Fell Pike	761958	651	98
Green Hill	702820	628	98
Gragareth	688793	627	98
Calf Top	664856	609	98
Brownber Head	845068	600c	91/92
Castle Knott	656841	538	97

Wharfedale and Littondale

Great Whernside	002739	704	98
Buckden Pike	961788	702	98
Fountains Fell (North summit)	864716	668	98
Fountains Fell (South summit)	869708	662	98
Yockenthwaite Moor	909811	643	98
Darnbrook Fell	884728	624	98
Sugar Loaf	894768	609	98
Birks Fell	916764	608	98
Horse Head	887780	605	98
Little Whernside	028776	604	98
High Green Field Knott	845784	602	98

Gunnerside Moor

Rogan's Seat	919031	672	91/92
Unnamed summit (West Moor) (Water Crag)	929046	668	91/92

NOTE: Most of the above summits are shown in greater detail on the Ordnance Survey Outdoor Leisure Maps, which are to a scale 1:25 000. Many of the features described in the routes that follow are more readily discernible using these larger scale maps, and walkers are strongly advised to use them in preference to the standard 1:50 000 series.

ROUTES

4.1 Whernside
4.2 Ingleborough
4.3 Pen y Ghent

The character of the Dales is fashioned wholly by limestone, the most dominant and conspicuous of rock types not only in the Dales but throughout the whole of the Pennines. It influences and determines the land forms, and impresses itself into the fine detail of the countryside, whether making its appearance in the grandeur of towering limestone cliffs, in the wide spread of limestone pavements, less noticeably in the tortuous catacombs that riddle the heart of the region, in the sinuous curving and moulding of riverbeds, or simply in the skill of men who have applied its qualities to construct walls and buildings everywhere.

The Dales are indeed limestone country, and possess in consequence a beauty that is unique and irreplaceable. The finest tracts of this remarkable region have been comprised within the Yorkshire Dales National Park, though some equally acceptable areas – Mallerstang, Wild Boar Fell, Middleton, Leck, and Nidderdale – which might have been included, have not.

Rough-hewn, the Dales lie sandwiched between (at their southern extreme) the Aire Gap, an ancient and natural pass, dominated by the town of Skipton, and the equivalent gap at the northern end, Stainmore Gap, now accommodating the A66 and the townships of Brough and Barnard Castle. To the west the Lune, for the most part, forms a readily identifiable boundary; less so the moorlands to the east which ultimately lose themselves in the Vale of Mowbray and the Vale of York.

Not everywhere however does limestone prevail. In a most delectable corner of England, the Howgill Fells are formed principally of slate, and their geological affinity lies with the Lakeland fells around Windermere. But the Lune gorge carves a boundary along the western and northern extremities of the Howgills which is both unavoidable and convenient, drawing the fells to the Dales country rather than the distant summits of Kentmere and High Street. These fells are rounded, unbroken, and distorted only by shadowy gullies that make gentle incisions into their sides; their tops are of turf, and their sides bereft of significant outcrops of rock. They stand aloof, smooth, curving domes that gather in a self-contained island of unenclosed, wall-free, untracked loveliness.

Other rocks prevail, too: gritstones, sandstones and shales, all tilted, faulted, eroded by ice, water and snow to form the landscape we find today. Isolated, flat-topped summits, once surrounded by living glaciers, maintain a uniform height, their smooth summits often capped by gritstone, and their sides given what has become a Dales profile, as hard Yoredale limestones project stubbornly through softer, more eroded shales.

Moving eastwards the Lune travels through Ravenstonedale, until we cross the Vale of Eden to meet the boundary of the national park high on the watershed above Birkdale, at the head of Swaledale. To the south and west the massive, lonely fells of Wild Boar Fell and double-topped Baugh Fell form a rewarding region for walkers, while the bleak fastnesses of Stonesdale Moor and Rogan's Seat are places where solitude is an appealing feature.

Further east the boundary of the national park nibbles tentatively at the outskirts of Richmond before pressing on south to Wensleydale. Beyond Coverdale and the high barrier formed by Carle Fell, Little and Great Whernside lies Nidderdale, inexplicably excluded from the national park, but offering some splendid walking in a truly wild domain. West across the summits, Wharfedale, by comparison, is a valley favoured by nature and enriched by romance, a narrow valley, cut by a crystal river and shut in by rolling pastures and sombre fells. From here a wide sweep passes north of Skipton, across the gathering grounds of the Aire, with its famed attractions of Malham Cove and Gordale Scar, and up into Ribble-country, dominated by the Three Peaks – Whernside, Ingleborough and Pen y Ghent. Less well known, the valleys of Kingsdale and Barbondale lead northwards into Dentdale, and so back to Sedbergh at the foot of the Howgills.

Ingleborough from Yockenthwaite Moor.

Everywhere the scenery constantly changes: limestone gives way to gritstone, craggy escarpments to soft-shouldered fells, and high, rugged mountains to wild, rolling moorland. Benign it appears now, but all around the evidence of the titanic struggle between the land and the elements is to be seen. Steep-sided gills, and cascading waterfalls (there are probably more waterfalls in the Dales than anywhere else in England) demonstrate the power of glaciers and water. Indeed, water is still a dominant feature, which makes it all the more remarkable that you will find only two natural water areas of any size, Malham Tarn and Semerwater – and the latter courting a legend suggesting it was the work of an angel who, rebuffed by the Druids who inhabited the region, repaid them by drowning them and their valley. So much for Christian compassion!

But the unique characteristic of the water in the Dales is its capacity suddenly to disappear underground, or with equal surprise, reappear in the middle of nowhere. It was the discovery that the Dales were hollow, honeycombed with miles and miles of caverns and underground passages, all formed by the abrasive action of water and the

Whernside and the Ribblehead viaduct.

limestone-dissolving capabilities of surface runoff, which almost had the Dales universally known as the Cave District; which, accurate as it may be, has something of an empty ring about it!

Understandably, then, this is a region that attracts walkers and non-walkers alike, something it can claim to have done for over eight thousand years, since the Mesolithic (intermediate Stone Age) people wandered into this part of the country. It was these early hunters who first started to alter the balance of things, initiating a change in the Dales that was to be most profound. Originally, the Dales would have been heavily wooded, but as New Stone Age (Neolithic) Man turned from hunting to farming so he began the clearance of the primeval forests.

Much later, by the time the Romans came, the Dales were part of a well-organised culture, the Brigantes, who fought for many years against the invading forces. Later still came the Saxons, the Danes and the Vikings, who cleared many of the valley bottoms for farming and homesteading, and left their legacy in the many corrupted place-names we find today. The Normans by comparison built castles at strategic points, Sedbergh, Skipton and Richmond, and developed new administrative centres, hunting forests and reserves. Monastic houses flourished at Fountains Abbey and Bolton Abbey, and set the pattern of the wool trade that was to follow.

But perhaps the most prominent feature of these times still remaining are the hundreds, probably thousands of dry-stone walls constructed under the Enclosure Acts of the eighteenth and nineteenth centuries by virtue of which land was allocated to local farms, often dispossessing the poorer farmers, ironically to work on the land as wall-builders. It was at this time that many of the present-day footpaths were created to facilitate opportunities for recreation, and to compensate for loss of access to the open hillsides and moorlands.

And so the story of the Dales goes on; the Industrial Revolution brought mills and mines and quarries the

Pen y Ghent

remains of which now delight the industrial archaeologist, while the botanist, geologist, ornithologist, rock climber, hill walker and nature lover have a vast array of interest set out at their disposal. True, the attention given to the Dales now by the status of national park has its disadvantages, but here are many quiet corners, many fascinating nooks and crannies, to ensure that there is always something for everyone. The latest invasion, tourism, is well under way.

Route 4.1 Whernside In spite of its superior elevation, Whernside (739816) is the least popular of the Three Peaks, such acclaim as it receives deriving from its association with the other two. It is also the least impressive in form, displaying none of the angular protrusions of the Yoredale Facies which are so prominent on Ingleborough and Pen y Ghent, and its unintrusive silhouette does nothing to arouse any suspicion that you are looking at the highest mountain in the Dales.

It is an elongated, narrow and rolling ridge that rises from the very outskirts of Ingleton to a summit guarded by numerous boggy stretches, and slips gently northwards, widening as it goes, into Dentdale. And though this gives

The final stretch to the summit of Whernside.

it the appearance of a beached whale, there is, on closer acquaintance, something about Whernside that brings walkers back, again and again.

Walkers wanting the most direct ascent will follow Routes 4.1b or 4.1f below, while the approach through Little Dale, almost travelling round to the north of the mountain before getting to grips with it, has a quiet charm only added to by the frequent to-ing and fro-ing of trains of railway enthusiasts along the justly popular stretch of the Settle–Carlisle line that passes across Ribblehead viaduct.

4.1a From Ribblehead by Little Dale Start along the broad track which leaves the B6255 at 764791, and follow this to the foot of the viaduct, a thing of wonder to my mind, being uneducated in engineering matters. The track continues beneath the arches, but follow instead a signposted path along the east side of the railway, past Blea Moor sidings and signal box, to cross Little Dale Beck, sometimes with difficulty, in the vicinity of a curious double bridge over the railway. The bridge carries not only the footpath but serves as an aqueduct for Force Gill as it flows from its gathering ground high up on Whern-

side, over its delectable little waterfall secluded in its own quiet ravine – a place to pause and admire the timeless beauty of water and rock – and on to join the River Doe near Chapel-le-Dale.

The path is signposted wherever there may be doubt, and once across the railway bridge further signs point the way to Dentdale, Dent Head and Whernside. The first noticeable ascent is engaged here as the path follows a fenceline to a stile, and beyond finally starts the westwards journey to meet the northern end of Whernside, using a wall marking the boundary between Cumbria and Yorkshire as a guide. The northern end of Whernside, dappled with small, shallow tarns (Whernside Tarns), is known as Knoutberry Hill, and here the wall bends southwards, above Greensett Tarn (not named on maps), and takes you unerringly across the summit and, for that matter, ultimately all the way down to Twistleton Scar End, near Ingleton.

DISTANCE: 6.5 kilometres (4 miles)
ASCENT: 435 metres (1430 feet)

From the summit, and especially along this approach, like many places in the Pennines there is a tremendous sense of space; splendid views open up, north-east across the head of Dentdale to Great Knoutberry Hill, round to Rise Hill backed by the mound of Baugh Fell, and the pudding-shaped Howgills leading the eye to the crumpled horizon of the Lake Mountains. Morecambe Bay sparkles over the intervening ridge of Gragareth and Great Coum, while the attention-commanding forms of Ingleborough and Pen y Ghent defy any attempt to let the eyes wander further afield to the south and south-east.

4.1b From Ribblehead by Gunnerfleet and Winterscales Leave Ribblehead as for Route 4.1a above, but

Ascending Whernside: Great Knoutberry Hill lies in the background (left).

stay on the broad track as it passes beneath the viaduct (watch for falling masonry – not an idle warning!) and continue to Gunnerfleet Farm, crossing Winterscales Beck by a bridge. Turn right after the bridge and continue on a metalled farm road to a T-junction; the road, right, leads to Winterscales Farm and, left, to Bruntscar, near Chapel-le-Dale. At the junction turn left and continue to a stile on the right at 751080. This same point may be reached via Winterscales Farm, avoiding the passage under the viaduct and continuing instead as if entering Little Dale to pass beneath the railway near Blea Moor sidings in company with a stream unimaginatively named Foul Gutter (not on the 1:50 000 map). Continue through the farm until you reach the stile.

From the stile the path ascends by a wall to the intake, and then in a straight line up a vertical quagmire to join the summit ridge three hundred metres from the top; turn right here. This route is well used (by the Three Peaks Walk, for example) but has little merit other than direct- ness and speed, neither of which are especially good reasons for tackling mountains, and, in this case, destined

Pen y Ghent from the slopes of Darnbrook Fell.

to tell you nothing about Whernside that will reward you in months and years to come.

DISTANCE: 4.2 kilometres (2.6 miles)

ASCENT: 435 metres (1430 feet)

4.1c From Chapel-le-Dale Start near the Old Hill Inn (743776) – a refreshing place to come back to in summer – and take the metalled track (Philpin Lane) which leads to Bruntscar Farm (739791), and here turn right to reach a stile giving access to a grassy meadow. (Note here, just before the stile, a gated bridleway signposted to Winterscales Farm; to ascend by Little Dale and descend to this point, returning to Ribblehead along this bridleway gives a satisfying round trip of 12.3 kilometres (7.7 miles).)

Cross the meadow to a stile, and then ascend to two more stiles straddling the intake wall. The route to the ridge is now by a sad flight of steps, originally intended to prevent erosion, but in need of attention themselves. Once on the ridge, its wall is encountered and should be followed up a series of boggy humps (the best going is usually on the very edge of the escarpment – but don't try this in winter!) to the summit.

DISTANCE: 4 kilometres (2.5 miles)

ASCENT: 445 metres (1460 feet)

4.1d By Scar End via Twistleton Hall Because there is nowhere to park cars conveniently, this approach to Whernside must start in Ingleton. It uses the Roman road (Oddie's Lane on some maps) on the north side of the River Doe.

Leave the main car park, near the community centre, and turn right under the disused railway viaduct and then left to descend to cross the River Doe. Take the first right after the river (signposted 'Beezley Farm Camp Site') and continue uphill to a gate (699745 – bearing a sign 'Twistleton Hall') and follow the farm road towards the prominent limestone outcrops of Scar End. The farm may also be reached by continuing on Oddie's Lane to a footpath (signposted 'Scar End') directly opposite the entrance to Beezley Farm, and following this as it eases across the fellside to the farm.

From the farm continue on the metalled roadway through a gate to gain an unmetalled track (Twistleton Lane) with open access on the right to the fellside. A short way beyond the farm take a conspicuous track rising diagonally across Scar End, which later doubles back to ease the ascent to the end of the long ridge descending from Whernside. As you climb above the limestone outcrops you come to a large cairn with walls some distance away, left and right. Make for the wall on the left, and follow this uneventfully all the way to the summit of Whernside.

DISTANCE: 10 kilometres (6.25 miles)

ASCENT: 625 metres (2050 feet)

4.1e By Scar End via the Waterfalls Walk The diagonal track ascending Scar End described in Route 4.1d may also be reached by an infinitely more picturesque route along the banks of the River Twiss as it descends from Kingsdale. The river, and its associated falls, however, passes through private land to which admission involves parting with money, but it is well worthwhile for the falls are among the most attractive in England. The waterfalls are well signposted in Ingleton and a car park found at the start of the walk.

Follow the well-trodden route alongside the river, which first passes through Swilla Glen to a series of fairly shallow falls, Pecca Falls, before ascending on a constructed walkway (past a small cabin selling food and drinks, and tickets – they get you at both ends!) to the major feature of the walk, Thornton Force. It isn't only the falls that are impressive, for here Kingsdale Beck plunges off the ubiquitous Carboniferous limestone on to the shattered, upturned edges of pre-Cambrian slates, and the limestones may be seen lying so close with the slates that a mere hand span will cover geological worlds more than 300 million years apart. I defy any thinking person not to be impressed by that!

The Waterfalls Walk, however, demands more than one price, for great care is required along the path. In recent years a number of young children, tempted away from the safety of the path, have fallen to their deaths in the narrow ravines, from which there is little chance of escape or survival.

At the upper end of the glen cross Ravenray Bridge and ascend the fellside beyond to gain Twistleton Lane at a gate. Turn right along the lane for a short distance in the direction of Twistleton Hall, and continue through another gate until you can ascend left to gain the diagonal track rising across Scar End. You can now follow Route 4.1d to the summit of Whernside; distance is marginally less, but the ascent is the same.

4.1f From Kingsdale The easiest, and the most uninteresting, ascent of Whernside is made from the Ingleton –Deepdale road, leaving the road at 721818 to ascend initially alongside the intake wall until a final dive may be made for the summit.

DISTANCE: 1.8 kilometres (1.1 miles)
ASCENT: 270 metres (885 feet)

Route 4.2 Ingleborough Viewed from the south-west, Ingleborough (741746) rises as an isolated summit from an extensive limestone plateau culminating in a fine series of scars overlooking Chapel-le-Dale. The mountain comprises a repeated succession of shales, limestones and sandstones – the Yoredale Facies – capped by a resilient

Ingleborough from Crina Bottom.

layer of millstone grit which has weathered to give Ingleborough its distinctive flat top, a feature easily identifiable from as far away as the western fells of Lakeland. Geologically it is a fascinating area; the whole limestone landscape is strewn with erratic boulders carried by glaciers, and riddled with caverns, shake holes and dry gorges where glaciation and melting water have fashioned fantastic forms out of the rock.

The dark summit of Ingleborough is surrounded by a massive encircling wall, containing the foundations, still traceable in the peaty summit, of many circular huts once part of a hillfort, Rigodunum, from where a Brigantian leader, Venutius, led a revolt against the Romans, a revolt finally quelled in AD 74 by Julius Agricola.

Ingleborough undoubtedly ranks as one of the most popular summits in the whole of the Pennines; it offers routes from all directions, has a splendid summit panorama, and seldom fails to repay the effort expended in achieving its lofty top.

4.2a From Clapham Clapham is a delightful Dales village, especially out of the tourist season when it displays a quiet rural charm. The ascent of Ingleborough from the village is by far the finest approach.

Start from the car park (746692) near the National Park Information Centre (the old manor house), and turn right to cross Clapham Beck by a stone bridge. Follow the sign for Ingleborough Cave, travelling along the beck which throughout its length is a favoured haunt of grey wagtails and dippers. There is an option, soon encountered, of entering the landscaped grounds of Ingleborough Hall Estate (an attractive proposition, for which there is a small fee) or of pursuing Clapdale Lane (signposted 'Ingleborough: Gaping Gill: Ingleborough Cave') to Clapdale Farm where a sharp descent, right, towards the beck will soon bring you to the cave.

Ingleborough Hall is now an outdoor centre, but was formerly the home of Reginald Farrer (1880–1920), a renowned botanist who made many journeys to far corners of the world in pursuit of his passion, and brought many plants back to Clapham. The grounds and the lake within them were created by the Farrer family in the nineteenth century. The estate is still privately owned. Further along the beck there are guided tours into Ingleborough Cave – but at this rate we will never reach our mountain, for more diversions await.

Clapdale Farm: Ingleborough.

▼ *Along Clapham Beck on the approach to Ingleborough.*

Follow the path beyond the cave. The valley bottom narrows dramatically and turns left to pass through the deeply incised jaws of Trow Gill, emerging via a rocky gorge into a hillocky no-man's-land before crossing a wall by a through-stile just as Ingleborough springs fully into view. A large pothole (Bar Pot) appears beyond the wall and to the left of the path, but the real treat lies a short way further on and off to the right. Here, surrounded by a

The entrance to Ingleborough Cave.

Trow Gill: ascent to Ingleborough.

fence, the innocuous Fell Beck is swallowed by the massive maw of Gaping Gill, reputedly large enough to contain St. Paul's Cathedral or York Minster (but not both!). The cave was first descended in 1897, and now on bank holiday weekends local caving clubs rig up a chair to lower ordinary mortals like you and me into the cave. With wry humour they will tell you there is no charge for lowering you down, but there is one for bringing you back up! If you do go down don't go wandering about; there are many branch passages off the main chamber to lead you astray.

From Gaping Gill the path heads north-west for Little Ingleborough (not named on the 1:50 000 map) which is gained by a steepish pull to a series of shelter-cairns and a fine view across Ribblesdale to Pen y Ghent and Fountains Fell. The continuation to Ingleborough's summit is without difficulty, the path passing through the hillfort wall before following a line of cairns to the summit trig, a massive cairn, and a crossed-wall shelter similar in construction to those on Helvellyn and Esk Hause in the Lake District. This shelter was erected by the Ingleton Fell

Rescue Team to commemorate the Coronation of Queen Elizabeth in 1953. The highest point of the summit, marked by another cairn, lies a few metres north-west of the trig, overlooking the Doe valley.

DISTANCE: 6.5 kilometres (4 miles)
ASCENT: 560 metres (1840 feet)

4.2b From Ingleton This ascent, though popular with visitors to Ingleton, is the least interesting of Ingleborough's ascents and serves better as a speedy descent for walkers who don't have to return to their starting point or who, having ascended Route 4.2a, don't mind the walk back along the road to Clapham, for example – this combination, incidentally, giving a splendid round trip suitable for a good winter's day.

Start from 701731 and ascend by the public bridleway across Storrs Common to gain a track (Fell Lane) running between walls to the fell gate near Crina Bottom Farm. The stream through the valley bottom beyond the farm is an excellent spot to find the fossil remains of the once overlying sea. The path continues ahead, rising steeply to gain the edge of the summit plateau in a series of peaty steps.

DISTANCE: 4.5 kilometres (2.8 miles)
ASCENT: 550 metres (1805 feet)

4.2c From Chapel-le-Dale Take the path (signposted 'Great Douk Cave') which leaves the B6255 at 744777 and follow it, ignoring the diversion to the cave, to the edge of the limestone pavement. Cross the limestone and make for two stiles over a wall. Beyond the wall the path rises more steeply, crossing a boggy section to the foot of the escarpment which has been prominently in view throughout the approach.

Ascend the steep escarpment, following a wall and taking care not to dislodge stones (the ascent is easier on the left), to a stile at the top from where the summit of Ingleborough can be reached by an obvious path through a final short rocky section. Once on the edge of the summit plateau the path fades, and locating the summit in mist can be tricky.

DISTANCE: 3.7 kilometres (2.3 miles)
ASCENT: 420 metres (1380 feet)

4.2d From Gauber Road Less well known than other lines of ascent this attractive ridge walk gives a fine approach to Ingleborough on days when other routes are congested.

Leave Gauber by the track (774785) to Colt Park and keep to the north-west side of the wall up Park Fell and on to Simon Fell where the path now skims along the edge of the escarpment until it joins Route 4.2c at the saddle between Simon Fell and Ingleborough.

DISTANCE: 5.5 kilometres (3.4 miles)
ASCENT: 420 metres (1375 feet)

Walkers seeking the summit of Simon Fell on this approach should leave the escarpment path at a stile (752757), and follow the wall upwards until forced to turn right by another wall as if to resume the journey to Ingleborough. The summit of Simon Fell lies unmarked along this dilapidated wall at 755752.

4.2e From Horton-in-Ribblesdale This ascent is simple, but largely uninteresting, though it is popular with walkers based at Horton and crosses some wild moorland high above Gaping Gill.

Start from the car park (808726) and leave by the wooden bridge across the River Ribble. Follow the road for 300 metres, to a bend, and there ascend directly ahead (signposted 'Crummackdale') past a row of railway cottages to the station. Cross the railway line and ascend to a narrow gate in the wall above, and continue across the field beyond. The route is then either obvious, signposted or waymarked (yellow spots on the rocks or yellow paint on posts), until it reaches the edge of the limestone pavement which it crosses in a straight line by an Iron Age track known as Sulber Nick.

Continue ahead across open moorland to a ruined shooting hut (767739) from where the path begins a lovely traverse across the southern slopes of Simon Fell until it rises with a final flourish to the rocky section mentioned in Route 4.2c, which it now joins for the short stretch to the summit.

DISTANCE: 7.2 kilometres (4.5 miles)
ASCENT: 490 metres (1610 feet)

Walkers who want to take in Simon Fell should descend to the saddle where routes 4.2c and 4.2d meet, and follow the wall north-east. To cross the summit, however, you must be on the northern side of the wall. It is worth nothing that a number of walls, many surmounted by fencing wire, meet on Simon Fell, and none are easy to cross, which does nothing to enhance the fell's already dubious appeal.

Route 4.3 Pen y Ghent Its two-tiered prow standing proud along the skyline, Pen y Ghent (838734) sails purposefully across the surrounding moorland like some ancient galleon, commanding a splendid panorama, and calling untold thousands to ascend its steep-sided flanks and tread its summit plateau. Its dramatic and powerful profile, especially on the approach from Brackenbottom, or when it rises pristine from the moors, wearing the white crown of winter, on a clear, blue-skied morning, gives it an appearance far greater than reality, for Pen y Ghent is the smallest of the Three Peaks. Its Celtic name derives, surely, from the Kingdom of Brigantia and the tribes forced into these remote regions by Roman and Teutonic settlers. But opinions differ as to its meaning. Generally thought to mean 'Hill of the Winds', but believed by others to mean 'Hill of the Border Country', its name unquestionably comes from the Welsh language in which the former would be *Pen y Gwynt* and the latter *Pen y Cant* – *cant* meaning a rim.

Pen y Ghent and the adjoining Plover Hill are not difficult summits to conquer, the higher peak lying plumb on the Pennine Way by which route it is conventionally ascended.

4.3a From Horton-in-Ribblesdale King Henry VI came to Ribblesdale during the Wars of the Roses (1455–85) to hide from his enemies, though it is far from a secluded spot these days, having tracks and paths radiating in almost every direction over the dales, and at the height of the summer season plagued with visitors who want to walk some part of the Pennine Way or tackle the Three Peaks Walk.

The ascent of Pen y Ghent from Horton is a simple affair, and leaves the B6479 at 808724, signposted 'Bridleway (Pennine Way)'. Follow the walled track to the fell gate near a ruined building close by which two potholes, Hunt Pot and Hull Pot, are well worth a diversion.

As you pass through the gate turn right and make for a narrow gate in a nearby wall, beyond which the gradually rising line of the route to the summit is never in doubt, even when it changes its easterly direction for a southerly one. The summit of Pen y Ghent is crossed by a wall, roughly north-east to south-west, and the summit cairn and trig point lie on the southern side.

DISTANCE: 4.5 kilometres (2.8 miles)
ASCENT: 460 metres (1510 feet)

4.3b From Silverdale Also using the Pennine Way, the ascent from Silverdale is by far the easiest line, only calling for bottom gear as you plod up the two final steep sections.

Start down the lane leading to Dalehead Farm (843715), an attractive photograph or painting with Pen y Ghent riding the skyline behind. The route continues to a prominent pothole, Churn Milk Hole, on the left of the path, shortly after which it bends, right, to traverse a long stretch of boggy ground. Much of this section has now been improved by grading the path or by the provision of boardwalks; this sort of attention can sometimes destroy the character of our moorland walks, but, quite frankly, it was never more desperately needed than along this route, and that ascending from Brackenbottom.

Continue to the foot of the prow, up which rises a crazy wall, and follow the obvious path to the edge of the summit plateau, where the wall, in mist, will guide you safely to the summit cairn.

DISTANCE: 2.5 kilometres (1.6 miles)
ASCENT: 270 metres (885 feet)

4.3c From Helwith Bridge A less well known, and therefore less crowded, route ascends from the B6479 at 814696 and takes a rising track, known as Long Lane, to Churn Milk Hole, where you should join Route 4.3b to the summit.

DISTANCE: 5 kilometres (3.1 miles)
ASCENT: 465 metres (1525 feet)

4.3d From Brackenbottom Brackenbottom lies along that little loop of minor roadway just south of Horton, by which it may be easily reached.

The route, which follows a wall throughout, is sign-posted at the start, and in its upper reaches elevated into a system of boardwalks and steps: these are badly needed here, for this route is often used as a descent by walkers having ascended Pen y Ghent from Horton by the Pennine Way. In its own right, however, it makes a fine, probably the best, approach, and gives, I feel, the most striking profile of the mountain.

Eventually, you will join Route 4.3b, just below the prow.

DISTANCE: 2.75 kilometres (1.7 miles) from Brackenbottom
ASCENT: 435 metres (1425 feet)

Walkers continuing to Plover Hill should gain the northerly side of the summit wall and follow a path accompanying the wall towards the lower summit. This path continues northwards, eventually, to Foxup Moor, but you will have to leave it as you approach the top of Plover Hill – walls continuing to be a guide – to reach the large summit cairn.

DISTANCE: 2.5 kilometres (1.6 miles)
ASCENT: 50 metres (165 feet)

Route 4.4 Blea Moor from Ribblehead An isolated and forgotten minor summit, Blea Moor (773826) is vastly overshadowed by Whernside. Yet it affords, for those who like that kind of thing, an energetic tramp through bleak countryside, well away from the masses – often a blessing on hot summer days.

Start along the broad track which leaves the B6255 at 764791, and follow this to the foot of the viaduct carrying the Settle–Carlisle railway line. At the viaduct take a signposted path along the eastern side of the railway, past Blea Moor sidings and signal box to a curious double bridge carrying both the footpath and the waters of Force Gill, a delightful waterfall secluded in a quiet recess of the hillside. At this point, just across the double bridge, the main track heads over into Dentdale – the Craven Way – or up on to Whernside, but you should leave the path and follow a fence, right, to a stile.

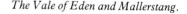

The Vale of Eden and Mallerstang.

Your route now takes you along the line of the Blea Moor tunnel, a remarkable feat of engineering, constructed in the 1870s, and burrowing under the moor for over 2 kilometres (almost 1.5 miles). Descend to recross Little Dale Beck, making for a prominent spoil heap ahead at which you will join a better trail ascending the hillside and passing two more spoil heaps and their air shafts which are 66,109 and 119 metres (217, 358 and 390 feet) deep, respectively, as you pass them. Shortly you will reach a boundary fence as the gradient levels, and here simply turn right for the summit trig.

DISTANCE: 5.3 kilometres (3.3 miles)
ASCENT: 240 metres (790 feet)

A return by the same route need not be contemplated by walkers with ample time to spare, the opportunity being at hand to extend the walk to the very head of Dentdale, returning to Ribblehead by an altogether different and quite acceptable route.

Return to the stile in the boundary fence, cross it, and continue ahead to a forestry plantation, still pursuing the line of Blea Moor tunnel, until you meet the railway line again at its northern entrance to the tunnel. From a stile drop down by the left side of the line, on a path that soon moves away from it through a gate to cross a footbridge. Downstream a short distance enter the farmyard of Dent Head by a pair of gates. Cross the bridge to the right of the buildings, and then make half right across a large field to a stile in the far bottom corner. Follow the right-hand fenceline to a farm bridge and on to the road through Dentdale at Bridge End Cottage.

Now turn right and ascend the road, passing under the arch of Dent Head viaduct. Continue with the road to a stile on the right at 786836, and there take an undulating track starting across Stoops Moss and making for High Gayle Farm where you should follow the intake wall round to Winshaw. Shortly afterwards you rejoin the B6255 for an easy return to Ribblehead. This last section, from Dent

Head, is part of the Dales Way, a splendid, meandering route aimed at making the most of the terrain, while the stretch of the B6255 you return on was an old coaching route from Lancaster to Richmond. Gearstones, nearby, was once an inn, patronised as much by the Scottish drovers as by local travellers.

DISTANCE: 14.3 kilometres (9 miles)

ASCENT: 385 metres (1265 feet)

Route 4.5 Great Shunner Fell Rising in splendid isolation from a massive area of wild moorland, Great Shunner Fell (849973) sends a long, curving spur southwards towards the upper reaches of Wensleydale. It is a line taken by the Pennine Way, a marvellous, natural route rising to a comparatively featureless summit, but one with a superb panorama. The Way links Hardraw (Hardrow) in Wensleydale and Thwaite at the head of Swaledale, and provides the principal lines of ascent. But walkers wanting to avoid the seemingly ubiquitous back-packing, mud-splattered wandering spirits of summer can make a perfectly acceptable ascent over Little Shunner Fell from the top of the Buttertubs Pass, *and* add Lovely Seat (Route 4.6) to the day's walking into the bargain.

The presence of the Pennine Way should not, however, lead you to underestimate Great Shunner Fell; it is a massive mountain, and good visibility a decided advantage that can only be dispensed with on the ascent from the Buttertubs Pass.

4.5a From Hardraw A cluster of attractive stone buildings, a couple of cafes, and reputedly the highest surface waterfall in the country without which Hardraw would be but a dot on the map, forms this tiny village along the fast-growing River Ure. As it is, no ascent of Great Shunner Fell should start (or finish) from Hardraw without your shelling out whatever is the going rate at the Green Dragon Inn to traverse the private grounds to the inner sanctum formed by the impressive cascade. It is a remarkable setting, a long, narrow, wooded ravine, once the scene of many open-air concerts (recently revived) in an acoustically splendid natural amphitheatre, at the end of which the waters of Fossdale Gill plunge freely into a dark pool. The surrounding undercut cliffs display in cross-section a part of the Yoredale Beds, the layers of material which lie above the Carboniferous limestone proper and beneath the younger millstone grits. And enterprising walkers, not afraid of getting a little damp, can walk behind the falls to obtain a unique view. But the pathway slopes and is slippery, and everyday shoes potentially lethal.

The way to Great Shunner Fell begins on the western edge of the village, taking the Pennine Way along a walled path to start before freeing itself from its confining embrace to tackle a succession of peat hags, pools, sink holes and rocky outcrops on the higher ground as you plod across wild upland to the trig and shelter on the summit.

DISTANCE: 7.2 kilometres (4.5 miles)
ASCENT: 480 metres (1575 feet)

On a clear day the far-reaching views are more than adequate compensation for the paucity of features nearby. Curiously Great Shunner Fell lies on the watershed between the rivers Swale and Ure, though neither of them rises within its compass.

4.5b From Thwaite Thwaite, its name meaning a 'clearing', is a reminder of the Norsemen who settled this region a thousand years ago. A group of strong, grey houses built of local stone in arguably the finest section of the Pennine Way, Thwaite was the birthplace of the famous naturalist brothers Richard and Cherry Kearton, and with the adjacent villages of Muker and Keld forms one of the most popular regions of the Yorkshire Dales, a frontier between sylvan beauty and the barren, windswept moorland reaches that give rise to the flowing streams and becks that are never far away. But with little scope for parking cars this is essentially walkers' country, and the ascent to Great Shunner Fell from Thwaite is one on which you must frequently look back the way you came to reap the full benefit of this magnificent upper section of Swaledale.

A short way north of the village a signpost steers you back along the Pennine Way, passing between boundary walls before finally reaching the intake at a gate. From here the path is clear enough, though boggy in places until finally it climbs to a prominent cairn on the north-east shoulder of the fell, from where it is only a short distance to the summit, finally reached by a stile over a fence which crosses the summit plateau.

DISTANCE: 5.3 kilometres (3.3 miles)
ASCENT: 430 metres (1410 feet)

The prominent lake seen to the north as you make for the cairn on the summit is Birkdale Tarn, created to serve smelting mills when lead mining was a major activity in this area. Lead was mined here as long ago as Roman times, and for nearly two hundred years to the latter part of the nineteenth century, forming a prosperous industry producing as much as 40,000 tons of lead annually. All that remains now are forlorn ruins, old shafts and adits, and the occasional derelict smelt mill chimney.

4.5c From Buttertubs Pass The route across the Buttertubs Pass is the relic of a very ancient track used primarily by farmers, drovers and travelling tradesmen, while the name Buttertubs derives from the group of potholes a short way down from the summit of the pass in the direction of Thwaite. Years of surface drainage have eroded the limestone into deep hollows where the water disappears into unseen fissures, and ferns, mosses and water-loving plants grow in stark contrast to the bleakness all around.

From the top of the pass, crossed by a fence, an alternative ascent of Great Shunner Fell may be made, taking in the minor summit, Little Shunner Fell, and largely avoiding the masses that tramp up and down the Pennine Way. The easiest ground, a little wet in a few spots, but infinitely drier than the Way, lies alongside the fence which shortly after the summit of Little Shunner Fell meets a section of wall, crossed easily enough. The fenceline links both the top of the pass and the summit of Great Shunner Fell, and is a safe and reliable, if occasionally indirect, route in poor visibility. In descent, remember to stay with the fence when the wall is encountered.

DISTANCE: 3.4 kilometres (2.1 miles)
ASCENT: 190 metres (625 feet)

Route 4.6 Lovely Seat from Buttertubs Pass This short ascent is unlikely to tax anyone unduly, though the mountain (879951) is significantly larger than might be imagined, with boundaries in both Wensleydale and Swaledale. A longer approach may be made from near Bainbridge, east along the A684, by crossing the River Ure and making for the broad shoulder flanked by Cogill Beck and Whity Gill, but there are numerous peat hags and bogs to make the going tedious and unattractive. The brief excursion from the Buttertubs Pass can easily be tacked on to a longer day over Great Shunner Fell.

Follow the fenceline from the top of the pass until this bears left, and then simply continue upwards, passing a number of large cairns, to the summit.

DISTANCE: 1.3 kilometres (0.8 miles)
ASCENT: 150 metres (490 feet)

Route 4.7 Great Knoutberry Hill Great Knoutberry Hill (789872) is the highest point of a massive, sprawling, unremittingly wild wedge of peaty moorland between Dentdale and Hawes; the whole area is generally known as Widdale Fell, flanking as it does along its northern side the valley of Widdale. North-east from the summit the land is a mess of peat groughs and weird peaty knolls that defy comfortable progress, and quite simply is just not worth visiting. I went: believe me! For the record, the insatiable, and disbelievers, the highest point of this morass is Little Knoutberry Hill, 599 metres, at 811889.

On a good day, however, the whole area is a fine vantage point, and ample justification for visiting Great Knoutberry. Two routes are available, suffering somewhat from neglect, but eminently worthwhile.

4.7a By Arten Gill Start from the narrow bridge (771859) where the minor road crosses the infant River Dee, and travel eastwards to pass under the massive railway viaduct on the Settle–Carlisle line. The viaduct is partly constructed of a black limestone, known locally as Dent marble, a rock once much prized for interior decorative purposes, especially as polished mantelpieces and ornamental columns. It isn't marble at all, of course, but a true limestone with a high carbon content. And though it may have gone out of fashion now, a river-washed piece of Dent marble makes a fine paperweight.

Beyond the viaduct follow the broad track, an ancient road from Arten Gill to Widdale, enclosed for a while on both sides by dilapidated stone walls, and crossed by a number of streams. High up on Cross Wold a second track heads left. This is Galloway Gate, used by Scottish drovers into the nineteenth century bringing cattle from the southern Scottish uplands to markets in Craven. Where the two tracks meet continue ahead, through a gate, the right-hand wall having now ended, and carry on a few hundred metres to a point where the remaining wall turns to ascend northwards up to the top of Great Knoutberry Hill.

The view from this point is quite impressive: Hawes and Wensleydale lie north-east while south-east the dark line of the Pennine Way can be picked out crossing the flank of Dodd Fell Hill. Walkers wanting to visit Wold Fell should head south here across initially wet ground before gaining more stable going as you approach the top of the fell.

For Great Knoutberry Hill simply follow the wall upwards to the large, uniquely shaped rectangular cairn sandwiched between the wall and a fenceline. A trig, marking the highest point, stands at the end of the wall, which here gives way to fences.

DISTANCE: 3.6 kilometres (2.25 miles)
ASCENT: 420 metres (1380 feet)

4.7b From the Coal Road The Coal Road is that minor road climbing from Lea Yeat, near Cowgill, over to Garsdale, and high up on Crosshills Wold it finds Galloway Gate heading off south-westwards to contour round neatly to the top of Arten Gill. From the gate, where Galloway Gate ceases to be a metalled roadway and becomes a stony track, the line of an old fence can be picked out ascending the hillside. Very little remains of the fence, though the Ordnance Survey Outdoor Leisure Map suggests something a little more substantial, but there are sufficient large posts remaining to serve as a reliable guide to the summit of Great Knoutberry. A newish fence encountered en route is so low as to let you pass without even needing to touch it.

DISTANCE: 1.3 kilometres (0.8 miles)
ASCENT: 170 metres (560 feet)

To construct a pleasant, short day's walk, ascend Route 4.7a, descend 4.7b, and then follow Galloway Gate back round to Arten Gill and the start. If you follow the fenceline descending north of west from the summit you will intercept Galloway Gate sooner than intended: the precise line of descent to the Coal Road requires a compass bearing in poor visibility before you meet the first of the fence-posts. The round trip will give a walk of 8 kilometres (5 miles), and the only ascent that for Route 4.7a.

Route 4.8 Dodd Fell Hill and Drumaldrace You could be forgiven for supposing that neither of these summits (841846 and 874867) would be likely to turn the mind to romantic lyricism. They rise like a pair of slumbering sentinels above the ancient market town of Hawes, waiting to trap the unsuspecting visitor, beguiled by the subtle attractiveness of this part of upper Wensleydale. On second thoughts, perhaps an unsuspecting visitor would fail to see the subtlety and the refined beauty, for these treasures await the walker with time to take it all in, time to observe these grand and bleak, brooding landscapes where the incautious traveller can so easily be mystified by the paucity of useful landmarks. Yet I confess to a strange affection for the place; there is something epic about the panorama that awaits the visitor to the top of Dodd Fell Hill from where the Three Peaks are seen from unfamiliar angles.

Both summits may be easily attained from the minor Hawes–Buckden road (Beggarman's Road) that climbs south from Hawes to join the Roman road from Ribblehead to Brough by Bainbridge (Virosidum). Where the road divides (861846) it is possible to park a few cars, and to reach Dodd Fell Hill by continuing in a south-westerly direction along the right branch of the road to North Gate (853841 – not named on the 1:50 000 map) and there heading north-west across rough ground to the summit trig.

DISTANCE: 2.5 kilometres (1.6 miles)
ASCENT: 105 metres (345 feet)

Drumaldrace, also known as Wether Fell, lies in the opposite direction, and involves returning along the road towards Hawes until you can leave it for the Roman road heading north-east. Continue along this enclosed track until, as the wall on the left ends, you can make directly for the summit, marked by a large cairn, across a short section of easy ground.

DISTANCE: 2.5 kilometres (1.6 miles)
ASCENT: 75 metres (245 feet)

There is, however, a much more satisfying way of combining the two summits, which begins by leaving Hawes on the Pennine Way, via Gayle. With the exception of the village centre the Way is clearly signposted, and high up on the northern slopes of Dodd Fell Hill, sandwiched between Widdale to the west and Sleddale to the east, deteriorates to a rough track. Follow this, climbing steadily, until you pass beyond the final intake wall ascending from your left, and there head across rough ground to the summit. You can delay your departure from the Pennine Way for another kilometre (0.6 miles) if the going underfoot is especially wet.

Leave the summit and, if you don't want to extend your walk by at least 4 kilometres (2.5 miles), head south-east to North Gate. Walkers with more time to spare, however, should return to the Pennine Way, aiming for a gate at 832841, near a ruined cottage, Rock Edge Cottage (shown but not named on the 1:50 000 map). Continue beyond the gate, still on the Pennine Way, to join the minor road at Kidhow Gate (830834), and turn left to follow the road, often drifted over in winter, around the southern perimeter of Dodd Fell Hill.

This circuitous journey may seem unnecessary, but it gives a tranquil traverse high above distant Langstrothdale and the nearby waters of Oughtershaw Beck which are the birthplace of the River Wharfe, and this alone is worth the extra effort. Travel along the road as if returning to Hawes, but at the start of the descent into Sleddale leave the road for the Roman road and Drumaldrace, as described above.

The quickest way back to Hawes is to return to the minor road and to descend via Sleddale. But good navigators should aim for a gate in a wall at 880874, beyond which a green path winds its way downwards to Burtersett. There are short cuts if time is pressing, all marked on the maps, and all evident, if faintly, on the ground.

The complete round trip, combining both fells, covers 20.5 kilometres (12.75 miles), and involves 510 metres (1670 feet) of ascent. This is not a walk to contemplate in poor visibility, though only the final section from Drumaldrace is likely to cause navigational problems. In any event it is a walk enhanced by the wide open spaces that typify the Pennines, and by the prevailing sense of truly being among the wild mountains.

Route 4.9 Hugh Seat and Lunds Fell by Hell Gill Beck The moorland summits at the southern end of the long and broad Mallerstang ridge possess none of the dramatic escarpments that are a predominant feature of the northern end. But they have their own quiet attractions to make this circular trip a pleasing excursion, well worth undertaking, and one you are quite likely to make in the company only of buzzards, kestrels, curlews, and such people as you may take with you.

Mallerstang is strictly the valley from the source of the River Eden northwards to Kirkby Stephen, the steep land on either side containing High Seat to the east and Wild Boar Fell to the west being known as Mallerstang Common. The origin of the name is given in Bulman's *Directory of Westmorland* (1885), in which the author advances the view: "This wild tract . . . was called Mallard Stang, the pool of the mallard, referring to some early expansion of the Eden." Through the valley the river continues northwards – one of only a few principal rivers of England to flow northwards – on its long journey to the Solway Firth. While to the south the waters flow into Wensleydale, and on to the North Sea, awarding to the comparatively insignificant section of upland covered by this walk the

▼ *Stone men on Wild Boar Fell.*

Looking down on the Vale of Eden.   ▼

distinction of lying on the watershed of England. The River Ure rises near the summit of Lunds Fell, close by a large square cairn on the edge of the southern summit of the fell, a mere hundred metres from the southernmost stream feeding the River Eden. For good measure the River Swale has one of its many feeders starting nearby, too.

A little distance to the north, across a stretch of peaty ground, trackless and wet, but neither impassable nor impossible, rises Hugh Seat (809991), named after Sir Hugh de Morville, one of the four knights who in 1170 took part in the murder of Thomas à Beckett, Archbishop of Canterbury. 'Seat' here, as in many places elsewhere, including the Lake District, derives from the Old Norse *saetr*, meaning a shieling or hill pasture.

By way of further distinction, the route follows for some distance the boundary between North Yorkshire and Cumbria, formerly between the North Riding of Yorkshire and Westmorland, and coincidentally the boundary of the Yorkshire Dales National Park.

Start, for ease of parking, at Cotegill Bridge (774969 – not named on the 1:50 000 map), and return along the road to Aisgill Moor Cottages. Here turn left to cross the Settle–Carlisle railway line, and then follow a broad track leading first to Hell Gill Farm and on to Hell Gill Bridge, where the gill forces its way through a deep and narrow chasm. Not long after crossing the railway, however, a short diversion to have a look at Hell Gill Force is well worthwhile; it is a splendid, miniature version (rather more picturesque, I think) of Hardraw Force, and gazes across the moor to a fine prospect of Wild Boar Fell and Swarth Fell.

At Hell Gill Bridge a broad, green track is encountered. This is marked on large-scale maps as The High Way, an old green road once a major route through the Pennines from Bronze Age times until the roadway was built during the last century.

(The High Way is sometimes known as Lady Anne

Clifford's Way, after the only surviving child of the third Earl of Cumberland and later Countess of Pembroke, who was famed throughout Westmorland during the seventeenth century for her extensive programme of castle renovations, in some instances in direct opposition to warnings from Cromwell himself. One such, Pendragon Castle, stands now in ruins in the mouth of Mallerstang, having had a troubled history since it was first constructed at the end of the twelfth century. The High Way begins at Cotter Rigg at the mouth of Cotterdale, on a line originating in Hawes, and travelling along the edge of Abbotside Common, across the watershed, and finally descending to join the road at Outghill, later recrossing the Eden at Pendragon Castle. It is a fascinating line, worthy of attention in itself, if the transport difficulties can be resolved.)

For the ascent of Hugh Seat, do not cross Hell Gill Bridge, but turn left for a few strides on the High Way, and then immediately right to follow the line of a wall ascending parallel with the unseen Hell Gill Beck. A short way further on the wall comes to an end, leaving you to continue along the course of the beck (now the county and national park boundary) until, just after an acute bend to the right (as you ascend the beck), the view ahead opens up for the first time, near a ruined sheepfold (795981), to reveal a prominent cairn ahead and above on the edge of Hugh Seat.

Continue along the beck, but only so far as the next stream joining from the right (east), and follow this until you feel disposed to break away from it to ascend directly to the first of two cairns on Hugh Seat, from where the second cairn (bearing an 1890 date and someone's initials) is easily gained. The cairn in its original state is, however, much older than this, having been erected in 1664 by Lady Anne Clifford, and is known as Lady's Pillar.

The highest point of the fell lies a short way further on, and is unmarked.

DISTANCE: 5.3 kilometres (3.3 miles)
ASCENT: 335 metres (1100 feet)

The continuation to High Seat, sticking in the main to the highest ground, sets off in a north-easterly direction, but soon swings to north-westerly as it approaches the summit.

DISTANCE: 2.6 kilometres (1.6 miles)
ASCENT: 45 metres (150 feet)

Lunds Fell lies almost due south, and the route to it is trackless. Walk southwards until you encounter a new fenceline, on the county boundary, paralleled by the old fenceline about one metre away, leaving a long thin no-man's-land, if anyone wants it! You can easily cross the fence, without damaging either the fence or yourself, at the point where it suddenly turns to head west, and from there simply stroll upwards to the double-topped summit, both marked by cairns, with the northerly summit being the higher.

DISTANCE: 2 kilometres (1.25 miles)
ASCENT: 45 metres (150 feet)

The head of the River Ure is marked on the map, and the nearby cairns are a pleasant resting place when the prevailing wind is not prevailing. From the cairns make a beeline for the Cotegill Bridge, which is in clear line of sight, and this will bring you back to the High Way a short distance south of Hell Gill Bridge.

Route 4.10 High Seat Sitting astride the boundary between Cumbria and North Yorkshire, and also forming the boundary of the Yorkshire Dales National Park, High Seat (802012) is the highest summit in the group of hills flanking the Vale of Eden and extending southwards to Dentdale and Garsdale. Yet for all its superior elevation it compares hardly at all with the likes of Wild Boar Fell, Baugh Fell, Great Coum and Gragareth. But it is the highest, and needs must when the peak-bagger drives!

The summit is most easily reached from the top of the Nateby–Keld road, starting from the parking space at the county boundaries. The journey simply follows the boundaries, and for that matter the watershed, south-west and then south, tackling a short, steep, wet, untracked and grassy section first to High Pike Hill before pursuing the highest ground southwards to High Seat itself; neither a difficult nor unduly long undertaking by any standards.

DISTANCE: 3.2 kilometres (2 miles)
ASCENT: 190 metres (625 metres)

Route 4.11 Nine Standards Rigg Theories abound about the origins of the nine massive stone pillars adorning the top of Nine Standards Rigg (825061); the number of theories merely serving to emphasise that no one really knows the truth. Certainly they appear on eighteenth-century maps, and have undoubtedly given the mountain its name. Some people suggest they were constructed to mark the county boundary (now North Yorkshire and Cumbria, pre-1974 the North Riding of Yorkshire and Westmorland), while local tradition has it that they were set up to delude an enemy – the Scots, presumably – into the belief that they were the standards of an encamped army. Occupying a commanding position overlooking the Eden valley they tend to support this claim, but reality is invariably more prosaic, and their construction in a straight line along the main watershed of England suggests some form of boundary mark.

4.11a From Hartley Part of the Coast to Coast Walk, the route from Hartley is more easily followed than that from the top of the Nateby–Keld road, though both are clearly shown on the 1:50 000 map.

Leave the minor road at the foot of Hartley Fell at 799075 and follow the bridleway as it ascends to join a wall above the valley below, Dukerdale (not named on the 1:50 000 map). The Nine Standards are prominent in view above, but do not be tempted to make a beeline for them, stay with the bridleway, formerly constructed to serve a group of small coal pits beneath the summit. After a while the path leaves the wall and ascends to pass the pits before curving north-eastwards, a little less distinctly once the pits are passed, to make for the summit plateau.

The summit is marked by a trig, but a morass of peat bars your way, necessitating a route to the Nine Standards first before doubling back to the trig, passing en route a viewpoint indicator erected by the Kirkby Stephen Fell Search Team in commemoration of the wedding of Prince Charles and Lady Diana Spencer. The indicator merely serves to underline what on a clear day is perfectly obvious: Nine Standards Rigg is a remarkable vantage point.
DISTANCE: 4.5 kilometres (2.8 miles) (from the road end)
ASCENT: 310 metres (1020 feet)

4.11b From the Nateby–Keld road Start from the parking space at the top of the road, marked by the county boundary signs, and resist the temptation of the narrow path leading from the rear of the space out on to the moor with the beckoning line of Coldbergh Edge in the distance; any approach by this route requires chin-length wellington boots, a rubber diving suit, an aqualung, plus waterproofs and a lot of faith!

Walk instead along the road (towards Nateby) for about two hundred metres until you can move right (a bridleway, shown on the map but less obvious on the ground) along the distinct division between limestone (on your left) and gritstone and peat (on the right). Follow this division, passing a line of potholes, Tailbrigg Pots, and a small tarn, finally curving round to the head of Dukerdale where Rigg Beck is neatly framed by the valley sides. Cross the beck and follow the wall round, northwards, until you leave it to make for a prominent shelter, just beyond which you will encounter the track ascending from Hartley, which should be followed to the summit.
DISTANCE: 4 kilometres (2.5 miles)
ASCENT: 145 metres (475 feet)

Route 4.12 Wild Boar Fell and Swarth Fell from the Vale of Eden The long valley containing the River Eden, flowing north, and the River Ure, flowing south, has always offered a gateway to the heart of the Yorkshire Dales, and has been an access used by Scottish raiders from the eleventh century onwards. It is still an active thoroughfare, linking Kirkby Stephen with Hawes by road, and Settle and Carlisle by rail.

The valley is flanked on the east by the long ridge of Mallerstang Edge, and on the west by a tremendous escarpment of gritstone rising to the summits of Wild Boar Fell and, to the south, Swarth Fell and its attendant, Swarth Fell Pike. These are lonely, windswept fells that nevertheless have great appeal, Wild Boar Fell in particular claiming to be the spot where the last wild boar in England was slain (in the fifteenth century by Sir Richard Musgrave). Other locations however – Crooke, near Windermere, and Kentmere, for example – also claim that infamous distinction. By far the finest way of experiencing the delights of Wild Boar Fell and its companions is to combine the two in an excellent and relatively quiet circuit, described here in an anticlockwise direction – the better, in my view – but perfectly acceptable t'other way round.

Begin from a small disused quarry near Cotegill Bridge (774969) where Near Cote Gill and Far Cote Gill meet in a picturesque waterfall at the back of the quarry. Walk down the road to Aisgill Farm and there turn left up a track passing under the railway viaduct, with a fascinating ceiling of stalactites. Turn right, after the viaduct, and pursue a path accompanying the intake wall which quickly appears. When, in a little over a kilometre, the wall bends right, bear half left, continuing along a line of potholes, Angerholme Pots, which have been with you for a while. There is no clear path along this section, but as you encounter limestone pavement take a course near its left edge which contrives to keep you free of the boggy ground further left.

It is impossible on a clear day not to be impressed by the superb escarpment ranging above you, the stone pillars of

Wild Boar Fell on the left prominent on the skyline, and the sharp, rocky silhouette of The Nab more directly above you. Continue along the edge of the limestone, aiming for the ridge at the northern end of the escarpment, which you can ultimately gain by a slanting path. Once on the ridge simply turn left and follow the crest of the escarpment to The Nab.

Strong walkers will find especial appeal in a more direct, unmarked line to The Nab leaving the moorland crossing at a point immediately beneath it and, in effect, going straight up. A short section of boggy ground needs to be crossed first, but, on firmer ground, start climbing steeply, aiming a little left of The Nab, to reach an unsuspected shelf containing an embryonic tarn and surrounded by towering outcrops of gritstone. The final pull to The Nab is again steep and a little loose, but should present no real difficulties.

Wild Boar Fell is one of those infuriating summits with multiple tops all of the same height. The traditional summit, marked by a trig and surrounded by a shelter, is reached easily from The Nab by a good path, and lies due south-west.

DISTANCE: 4.8 kilometres (3 miles)
ASCENT: 390 metres (1280 feet)

The second height lies due east of the trig, on the edge of the escarpment, while the third is among the conspicuous stone pillars (increasing in number every year) a short distance further south, also on the edge of the drop to Mallerstang Common. As on the flat top of High Street, near Kentmere in Lakeland, the summit plateau of Wild Boar Fell is said to have been used for horseriding, wrestling and athletic sports.

There is no difficulty in continuing to Swarth Fell, providing you remember to head south-west from the stone pillars in order to circle around Aisgill Head on a narrow path, rather than trying to make a beeline. The path descends to a broad col between the two mountains, housing a pleasant tarn, and a new fenceline proves useful in poor visibility to guide you to a wall (the county and national park boundary) coming up from Uldale, which continues upwards to cross the top of Swarth Fell. The summit of Swarth Fell, however, lies 100 metres east of the wall, and is marked by a large cairn.

DISTANCE: 2.5 kilometres (1.6 miles)
ASCENT: 80 metres (260 feet)

A good path leaves the cairn, heading for the minor top, Swarth Fell Pike, but in poor visibility the wall, and a new fenceline which ensues, may again be used as a guide.

There are two large cairns, reached by step stiles, near the fence on top of Swarth Fell Pike, and from the second (and lower) of these you should descend, not too steeply, to cross boggy ground to reach either Near or Far Cote Gill, which then steer you back to the quarry starting point. The small waterfall at the back of the quarry may be passed by descending a corner on the left as you go down.

DISTANCE: (Round trip) 10.5 kilometres (6.6 miles) (depending on line taken)
ASCENT: 470 metres (1540 feet)

Route 4.13 Great Coum and Gragareth Great Coum (701836) is the northernmost and highest point of a splendid ridge marking the boundary between Lancashire and Cumbria. It is an excellent vantage point, with splendid views over the Yorkshire Dales, the coastal plain of Lancashire, and as far as Lakeland. Yet it lies in an area seldom visited, except by that species of humanity who pursue their pleasure under the hilltops rather than on them.

4.13a From Leck The approach from Leck facilitates a pleasing circuit to be made in what is a corner of Lancashire unknown, I suspect, to the vast majority of Lancastrians. Leck lies just off the A65, a short distance south-east of Kirkby Lonsdale, and close by Cowan Bridge. Cowan Bridge itself owns a certain notoriety as the site of the school for clergymen's daughters attended by the Brontë sisters. The original school building, immortalised in Mrs. Gaskell's biography of Charlotte and as Lowood in *Jane Eyre*, though altered, is still there (it's now a row of terraced cottages), a plaque commemorating its place in history. The school was moved to Casterton in 1833.

Cowan Bridge, and Ireby a short way further south, both afford access to Leck, and from there to a metalled roadway running into the great hollow of the hills as far as Leck Fell House. The division of maps puts this area on two sheets, 97 and 98, though the latter may be discarded in favour of the Outdoor Leisure Map for the Western Area of the Yorkshire Dales; a different scale, but an infinitely better production. There are two ample parking areas near Leck Fell House – still an active farm – and you should begin from there. There are no legitimate access routes on to the hills, but well-behaved walkers have enjoyed unrestricted use for years. Don't be alarmed then if you are approached by a local farmer enquiring whether you have a permit; it's the potholers he is concerned about,

On Wild Boar Fell.

especially those without proper authority to enter the many systems that permeate the ground beneath your feet.

Begin along the road to a gate on the right just before Leck Fell House, beyond which a broad track heads out across the lower slopes of Gragareth. You can follow this track for a short distance, if you wish, or take immediately to the hillside. Either way your immediate objective is the stand of three stone pillars, the Three Men of Gragareth, prominent from where you left the car, but not from the track below them. It is presumed the pillars were constructed by the men who built the stone wall you will find along the summit ridge.

From the Three Men head east over easily sloping ground until you either hit the trig point marking the highest point, or the wall beyond. The trig stands about two hundred metres from the wall and could be missed in poor visibility.

To continue to Great Coum simply follow the wall, a remarkably well-constructed and unusually high affair that might have been intended to keep Lancastrians and Yorkshiremen apart in days gone by. On the east side of the wall many more walls ascend from Kingsdale, but the western side is free of these impediments to progress. As a result you can stroll easily over the intermediate top, Green Hill, its summit unmarked, all the way to Great Coum, having to negotiate only one wall, and that by a convenient gate.

Just beyond the gate, where its wall and the ridge wall meet, you will find the County Stone, a large, primeval boulder where the old counties of Lancashire, Westmorland and West Riding met.

The top of Great Coum is adorned by an impressive and large cairn. It stands on the north side of the ridge wall, and there is no easy way to it now that gaps in the wall have been repaired. But let me assure you, the cairn does not mark the highest point of the hill, this distinction being accorded to the spot height (687 at 701836) which is unmarked on the ground. Unfortunately this lies in an altogether different hill enclosure, and is just as inaccessible, except from the Occupation Road (Green Lane on the maps).

By moving west from the top of Great Coum, still following the wall, you will eventually find gaps, if you want to visit the tall cairn. But by then you will have spotted another fine cairn perched on the brink of a small outcrop, The Crag, and overlooking virtually the whole of Dentdale. This is a fantastic spot, and a super place for lunch.

To return to Leck Fell House, continue along the wall to Crag Hill, and from there descend across untracked ground to the confluence of Long Gill and Ease Gill. Ascend gradually from the becks, aiming for the intake wall above Ease Gill where you will pick up a narrow path which leads in due course to the broad track on which you started this round. The return to the start is a simple stroll.

DISTANCE: 11.5 kilometres (7.2 miles)
ASCENT: 360 metres (1180 feet)

4.13b From Dentdale This approach, too, is quite splendid, though it is shorter, involves more ascent, and the views are a little more restricted until you reach the top of the hill. Nor is it convenient to include Gragareth if you have to return to Dent.

Leave Dent by the path that courts Flinter Gill, a splendid access that climbs easily to the Occupation Road. The path can be found at the head of the minor road ascending away from the car park, toilets and picnic area in the village centre, tucked away behind an attractive group of cottages. On arriving at the Occupation Road turn right for a short distance – the track continues westwards to join Barbondale Road, and so, of course, you can ascend from there, too – and then head south on a track aiming for Crag Hill until this gives on to the open hillside. Great Coum now lies south-east, and you can more or less make a beeline for it, or at least for the tall cairn everyone thinks is the summit!

DISTANCE: 4.5 kilometres (2.8 miles)
ASCENT: 540 metres (1770 feet)

You can return to Dent by heading south from Great Coum to the County Stone, from where you can descend eastwards to the Occupation Road, reaching it more or less level with the attractive falls at the head of Gastack Beck, and then heading north until you can return by Flinter Gill. Or you can do th'ole lot, t'other road round!

Route 4.14 Baugh Fell Pronounced 'Bow' as in 'bow-tie', Baugh Fell (741916) is a juggernaut of the Pennine mountain world. Covering a vast area of some 47 square kilometres (18 square miles), it is a mountain that you either like or dislike, it's far too big simply to ignore. And sooner or later every self-respecting walker is going to wonder about Baugh Fell.

In words of discouragement, Baugh Fell is described by Wainwright as "desolate" and "a vast wilderness", by Colin Speakman, a man who lives and works in the Yorkshire Dales, as "a most formidable and frankly dreary hill, a boggy and empty wasteland", and by Walt Unsworth as "a prime contender for the dubious honour of being the most boring hill in the Pennines". Paradoxically, all three writers then went on to find something nice to say: Wainwright describes "attractions in plenty . . . and hidden beauties revealed only to those who search for them on foot"; Speakman says that "the views from the huge summit plateau, with its shallow tarns, are good and most certainly worth the effort of getting there", while Unsworth, still unsure of himself, considers that "It is the sort of place where the journey is everything and the goal nothing." All three are experienced and talented writers, but here I could almost believe their spirits have been suppressed by what their eyes have seen and their legs have felt – if I didn't know better! Surely, as walkers we commune with all our senses.

Baugh Fell is one of three summits between the How-gills and the Vale of Eden, and the other two, Wild Boar Fell and Swarth Fell, are considerably better known. No approach is feasible from much of Garsdale to the south, countless walled enclosures making access a difficult task. And the undoubtedly beautiful approach through Grisedale, a remote and isolated valley, is now made difficult, particularly for the motorist, by active dis-couragement in the form of numerous No Parking signs that have sprouted by the roadside in recent years. Walkers who still want to experience the delights of this approach should follow the footpath from Garsdale road, opposite the turning to the station, to Moor Rigg and from there to Round Ing where the open fell is finally encoun-tered. Continue ahead for a little over a kilometre until, on the watershed between Grisedale and Uldale, you can ascend south over untracked ground to the summit.

Just as beautiful is the approach along the Rawthey, following the river to its source high on the fell. Near where the Rawthey passes beneath the A683 at Rawthey Bridge (713979) there is a large parking space, and just across the road a rough track known as The Street, once the main road between Sedbergh and Kirkby Stephen, swings away from the Rawthey. Follow this for approxi-mately half a kilometre until a second track heads east across the moorland, more or less parallel with the Raw-they. There is an earlier turning, within minutes of the start, which will take you to the same place, but this is a narrow and indistinct path and can easily be missed.

As you follow the infant river its valley becomes narrow and steep-sided, and you enter a world of intrigue and natural beauty as you are led through secret hollows, by cascading falls – Uldale Force in particular is grand, but difficult to see and dangerous to approach – and on to a fine curving gorge called Dockholmes (not named on maps). Once beyond Uldale Force you can follow the bed of the stream to a certain extent, but spate conditions and the occasional rocky barrier will force you to find alternative, higher routes. High to the north-east, Swarth Fell rises as a massive backcloth to a scene that is constantly changing, until finally you reach a major change in the direction of the stream, Rawthey Gill Foot. Here continue southwards with the gill to an attractive junction between Rawthey Gill and Swere Gill, and take your choice, either gill leading you to the summit plateau across which a wall runs roughly east to west, effectively preventing you from going too far.

Maps and writers try to give Baugh Fell two identities, East and West, though one is quite sufficient and proper. Rawthey Gill leads you to a trig station on Knoutberry Haw, generally considered to be the highest point, but Tarn Rigg Hill, a kilometre to the east, is two metres higher. Your approach by Swere Gill, making for two prominent cairns on the skyline, takes you first into an area of shallow tarns, contained by the cap of millstone grit that here lies on top of layers of sandstone and shale. The summit is unmarked; it lies over the wall, near a slight kink in an otherwise uninterrupted line of stonework.

DISTANCE: 8 kilometres (5 miles)
ASCENT: 470 metres (1540 feet)

Return by crossing to Knoutberry Haw and descending easily northwards to West Baugh Fell Tarn, and from there head north-west down a long tilted carpet of open moorland, or slightly more to the west to Taythes Gill, marked by a small area of woodland, for more cavorting with narrow, steep-sided ravines and waterfalls before rejoining The Street for the short walk back to Rawthey Bridge.

Route 4.15 Castle Knott and Calf Top Rather like that splendid group of Lakeland outcasts sandwiched between the M6 and the A6, the grassy ridge culminating in Calf Top (664856) has undoubtedly been neglected by reason of its failure to achieve that magical mystery height, 2000 feet: at 609 metres it fails by 2 feet! More's the pity, because this is an enjoyable walk with arguably the best views in this extremity of the Dales.

Begin near Barbon Church where a path (signposted 'Public Footpath') shares the access to Barbon Manor. Cross Barbon Beck and as the roadway bends to the right head north across Barbon Park to follow the edge of a small copse to an iron gate. This section is untracked and can be very wet. From the gate cross a small enclosure to the south-eastern corner of Eskholme Farm where a collapsed wall ascending the hillside will guide you to a gate in the intake wall.

Eskholme Farm may be reached by a drier route, using the farm access road from the minor road running north out of Barbon. Behind the farm buildings a stone staircase leads neatly to a stone stile with a tiny wooden gate, the collapsed wall now ascending on your left.

Beyond the intake wall the path disappears until you pass Eskholme Pike, and then two appear; one staying on the highest ground, the other paralleling the wall on your right. This section is initially steep, but easier ground is not far away, and the traverse to Calf Top, passing first over Castle Knott, is uneventful in itself but bestowed with a stunning drop into Barbondale and tremendous views seaward that on a good day will stretch from Blackpool Tower to the shipyards of Barrow.

DISTANCE: 5 kilometres (3.1 miles)
ASCENT: 560 metres (1835 feet)

Do not be tempted to descend either into Barbondale – there is only one bridge across the beck, and this is due south of Castle Knott – or into Dentdale – no rights of way exist and the gradient is dangerously steep for a good stretch of the ridge. Either return along the ridge, or continue round Long Bank and follow the right of way down to Fellside, reaching the A683 near the Middleton Fell Inn. You are then faced with 6.5 kilometres (4 miles) back to Barbon along the minor road.

An ascent from Middleton Fell Inn involves 7.3

kilometres (4.5 miles) and 510 metres (1675 feet) of ascent, the track setting off just on the north side of the inn.

Route 4.16 Great and Little Whernside from Wharfedale Although most easily and more frequently ascended from Kettlewell in Wharfedale, Great Whernside (002739) and its peaty companion form the head wall of Nidderdale, a wild, captivating and worthy lieutenant of

The summit plateau of Great Whernside.

▼ *The summit of Great Whernside.*

the Yorkshire Dales National Park, yet inexplicably excluded from it. Rising little more than a kilometre north of Great Whernside's highest point, the Nidd wends its way eastwards through some of the most desolate, high moorland in the Pennines, flowing en route through Angram and Scar House Reservoirs before turning south to seek less inhospitable surroundings. This is far from easy fell-walking country, but the simple, curving lines and unadulterated, windswept bleakness lend it, in early spring or late autumn, an awesome beauty that penetrates the soul.

By contrast, Wharfedale is an animated thoroughfare, popular, and unashamedly beautiful. Through its midst flows the seductively attractive River Wharfe, probably one of very few English rivers to possess its own Roman goddess, Verbeia, described on an altar found in Ilkley as the goddess of the Wharfe. Yet for all her undoubted beauty (if the river is any testament) she must also have had her dark side, for the river, too, in spite of its humble beginnings high up on distant Cam Fell, is in places treacherous and fierce, with a record for more deaths by drowning than any other river in the Dales.

'Whernside' – from the Old English, *cweorn-side* – means the hill from which the millstones come, and a few

Great Whernside from the head of Coverdale.

Buckden Pike from Great Whernside.

still scatter Great Whernside's slopes, forlornly telling of an arduous by-gone age. One is led to assume that the millstones of *Great* Whernside were simply of larger dimensions than those of Whernside, of Three Peaks fame, which mountain is somewhat higher. And walkers who visit the boggy summit of Little Whernside will be hard pressed to believe any form of rock exists there at all.

4.16a From Kettlewell by Hag Dyke

Kettlewell, a former lead-mining village and a quaint study in grey and green, sits at the confluence of the Wharfe and a minor tributary, Cam Gill Beck, which greedily gulps the many side streams and cascades issuing from adjoining slopes. Sheltered on the north, east and west by high fells, Kettlewell, even in the depths of winter is noticeably warmer than many neighbouring villages. "The charm of Kettlewell is abiding," wrote Professor F. W. Moorman over sixty years ago, "the village seems the peculiar abode of peace and quiet beauty . . . the limestone terraces, with the fringes of hazel and rowan coppices, give to the district a characteristic beauty."

You enter the village from the south by crossing the Wharfe, and immediately encounter, on your left, a river-bank car park run by the National Park authority. Leave the car park, heading into the village, and cross the beck to turn right in front of the Bluebell Hotel (established in the seventeenth century) to follow the course of the beck. At a road junction (Post Office on the right), keep ahead on the minor road to Leyburn, but in a short distance, where the Leyburn road bends sharply left and tackles a 25% gradient (1 in 4 in old English!), keep ahead again, shortly descending, right, past a church, to cross the beck again.

Over the beck, turn left on a broad track to a signpost indicating the way to Hag Dyke and Providence Pot. The beck on the right here (unnamed on the 1:50 000 map) is Dowber Gill Beck, the source of which, high beneath Great Whernside's summit, saw much lead-mining activity in years gone by. The main track, above the ravine of Dowber Gill, is an easy gradient, and leads uneventfully to Hag Dyke, a Scout hostel, established in 1947.

Pass in front of and then around the hostel to cross the wall at the rear by a stone stile, and ascend left up the rock-strewn hillside which ensues. A small plateau encourages a breather before the final slopes to the summit of Great Whernside. Much millstone grit abounds here, and the summit is marked by a large cairn and trig. The view is

Kettlewell and the Wharfe valley.

magnificent in all directions, possessing the sort of spaciousness only found in Scotland and a few parts of central Wales.

DISTANCE: 3.8 kilometres (2.4 miles)

ASCENT: 500 metres (1640 feet)

4.16b From Kettlewell by Top Mere Road and the Coverhead Pass Considered by many to be the finest, if a roundabout, route to Great Whernside, this approach spends a long time circling the mountain before sneaking up on the blind side, and only then, in my view, rather tamely; most of the effort is spent reaching the Coverhead Pass.

Leave Kettlewell as for Route 4.16a until you reach the 25% gradient road for Leyburn, which you must now tackle, but only for a short distance, until, as the minor road bends sharply right, you can continue in a northerly direction up a broad track (signposted: 'Cam Head'). Follow the track as it curves eastwards to prehistoric Tor Dike (sic) near the top of the Coverhead Pass. Cross the Leyburn road and descend slightly to a yellow gate in a wall (signposted: 'Scar House Lodge'), but once through the gate continue ahead (ignoring the bridleway sign) to ascend the northern shoulder of Great Whernside. There is no right of way here, but a good path suggests that open access is tolerated, as in many parts of the Dales, providing no damage is done to walls and enclosures, or to animals.

The approach to Tor Mere Top.

Thinking about the final pull to Tor Mere Top.

Once at the top of the shoulder it is a short walk, passing a large compartmentalised stone shelter facing east, to the summit of the mountain.

DISTANCE: 7.7 kilometres (4.8 miles)
ASCENT: 525 metres (1720 feet)

4.16c From the Coverhead Pass By far the shortest and simplest line of ascent, there is little to commend this approach by itself. But for a very short day, drive to the top of the Coverhead Pass, a delightful prospect, especially as you approach Park Rash, and from there follow the yellow gate route described in Route 4.16b.

DISTANCE: 2.6 kilometres (1.6 miles)
ASCENT: 210 metres (690 feet)

The continuation from the summit of Great Whernside to Little Whernside, while starting off with great aspiration, curving above the headspring of the River Nidd, promises in the end only to deceive. Move north from the summit, as if descending to the Coverhead Pass, but, where the path to the top of the pass drops to the left, continue along the line of a wall (and the National Park boundary) to the col between the two mountains, shortly after which the wall departs for Coverdale, leaving you with a fence for the remainder of the journey to the most easterly 600-metre summit in the Pennines. Until the final rise to the

top the going is not too bad, but it ends in a glorious
eruption of peaty pustules that can appeal, surely, to no
one; though hill-walking eccentrics like me have had
lunch and half an hour's sunbathing in late March up
there!

DISTANCE: 5.5 kilometres (3.4 miles)
ASCENT: 80 metres (260 feet)

The summit of Little Whernside lies somewhere due east
of the junction of two fences. Though there is a cairn north
of one fence, higher ground undoubtedly rises to the south
and east, but quite which crown of heather has the advantage is far from clear and likely to change with the next
severe storm.

Route 4.17 Great Whernside from Nidderdale The upper reaches of Nidderdale are by any standards wild and
uncompromising walking; no easy Sunday strolls here
unless you stay close by the reservoirs. Challenging is a fair
description. And rewarding, too, if you contemplate the
rolling vastness with an eye for fine, soaring fellsides and
the glint of sun on peaty becks, or understand the com-
panionship of solitude. Once described as "the modest
maiden of the Pennine dales, and an altogether delightful
region for those who love Nature in her softer moods",
Nidderdale does indeed have a gentleness that contradicts
its own harshness, as if these two opposites have found
harmony in this neglected corner of England. Inexplicably, Nidderdale, as satisfying a dale as any, has been
excluded from the Yorkshire Dales National Park, but is
perhaps in many ways the better for the lack of attention
bureaucracy seems invariably to bring.

It takes an energetic soul to undertake the 'Nidderdale
Round', as I might term it, starting by the dam of Scar
House Reservoir and pursuing an ancient pathway to the
col between Great and Little Whernside, and descending
from the summit over the desolation that is Riggs Moor.

A car park with adjoining heated (!) toilets lies close by

the dam, and the road to it is followed from the village of Lofthouse where the access to the water authority's lands are clearly identified. There is a toll for using the car park, one you pay at the start of the road, not at the car park, so don't be caught out.

Sadly, reservoirs have been guilty in parts of the country of destroying beautiful landscapes, and they have effected radical changes in the scenery of the Pennine Dales. Thankfully those that occupy Nidderdale serve only to complement the landscape. Gowthwaite, lower down Nidderdale, in particular, has become famous as a haunt for an amazing variety of bird-life. The two reservoirs in Upper Nidderdale, Angram (completed in 1914) and Scar House (1936), are no exception to this satisfying scene. Only the dams intrude, and not disastrously so at that.

Begin then from the car park and cross the dam of Scar House Reservoir to turn left on a rough track, Carle Fell Road. This is an ancient market road by which cattle drovers, packhorse men, traders and customers would travel to markets and fairs at Masham. Where this track climbs northwards to cross into Coverdale, a less conspicuous path continues westwards to the col between Little Whernside and Great Whernside. Follow this, across the lower slopes of Little Whernside to the wall on the col, and then simply follow the wall until, by chance close by the tiny spring that is the source of the River Nidd, it turns abruptly to the west to the top of Coverdale Pass. Here head slightly east of south to the trig among the outcrop of rocks on the summit.

You must now continue roughly south, along the highest ground if you wish to avoid some broad muddy expanses, to a cairn (006733) near a fenceline, and then follow the fenceline east to a small pile of stones (019736) near the point where the fenceline dog-legs right. Leave the fence at this point to make for the south side of Angram Reservoir, by way of West Gill Dike, part way along which you will encounter a wet path heading east to ease your progress somewhat. This peters out near a wall which you follow down to the reservoir's edge. Alternatively, you may follow the stream down to the weir at the southern inflow to the reservoir. A broad track along the water's edge leads to a metalled roadway linking the two dams.

It has to be said that the section from the top of Great Whernside to the Angram Reservoir is among the toughest going in the whole of the Pennines. No pathways help your progress, and the terrain can be summed up in one word – ankletwistin'boneshakin'kneewreckin'Godforsakenbogcountry! But it has its fascination. Honest!
DISTANCE: (Round trip) 18.5 kilometres (11.5 miles)
ASCENT: 375 metres (1230 feet)

Route 4.18 Buckden Pike Buckden Pike (961788) is a homely hill, as much a part of Buckden village as the cottages and shops themselves. It is, even in the depths of winter, a favourite walk to stroll along the Rake, a wooded path easily ascending obliquely across the lower slopes of the Pike, by which way one of the routes that follow begins.

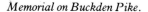

Memorial on Buckden Pike.

Buckden, once the centre of a vast hunting forest in medieval times, is a fine starting point for walkers, every direction offering a store of those pleasing pictures which are the joys of Wharfedale, and indeed of much of Dales country: brief glimpses of bubbling becks, tree-lined ravines reminiscent of Scotland, distant airy views of village houses and farm buildings gathered neatly on hillsides, the play of sunlight on angled grey roofs – each bringing its own rewards and the sense of freedom for which we take to the hills. Yet Buckden has a somewhat bemused air about it. Perched on a hillside at the meeting of three ways – the road from Langstrothdale, the road north over Kidstones Pass into Wensleydale, and the road along the dale itself – it is as if the village can't quite decide whether it is a centre to which the life of the upper dale is drawn, an objective for those lower down the dale, or a launch site for travellers heading over the pass. However you see it, as a visitor, Buckden is a delightful place, well worth a day's exploration in itself.

4.18a From Buckden At the northern end of the village a National Park car park has at one end a gate giving access to Buckden Rake, and you should start along this. As you leave the sparse trees of Rakes Wood behind – a splendid view here of Hubberholme and the upper dale – the track turns right through a gate. At the next gate fork right and resume the upward climb through a succession of gates and pastures until finally you are contained by a wall and effectively directed upwards to the trig and large cairn on the summit.
DISTANCE: 3.5 kilometres (2.2 miles)
ASCENT: 460 metres (1510 feet)

4.18b From Starbotton More than most Wharfedale villages, perhaps, Starbotton has kept the air of a lead-mining place. Its houses are more sparing of space than in purely farming villages, and give Starbotton its individual character.

Lying half way between Buckden and Kettlewell, it is a wonder that Starbotton survives at all, since in 1686 its position, close to Cam Gill, brought disaster as in a few minutes a terrible storm turned the becks into torrents pouring down the hillside. One old record recounts, "the rain lasted 1½ hours, the hill on one side opening, and casting up water to a prodigious height." Starbotton, many of its houses but recently built, took the full force and was almost swept away; cottages were knocked down, while those that remained were filled with mud and water, and acres of fields covered with mud and stones.

Near the Fox and Hounds (rebuilt in 1834 in the Georgian style), follow the line of Cam Gill Beck to a bridge, and cross this to ascend Walden Road, passing evidence of lead-mining activity en route, to a bridlegate at a sharp angle in a wall. Pass through the gate and ascend a slope, left, to a memorial cross erected by a Polish airman, the lone survivor of a plane crash in 1942. From here it is an easy walk to the top of Buckden Pike, its wall crossed by a stile.

DISTANCE: 4.7 kilometres (2.9 miles)
ASCENT: 475 metres (1560 feet)

The summit of Buckden Pike.

The facility to cross the River Wharfe by a footbridge, gained by a path just south of Starbotton, enables you to make a pleasant circular walk, ascending Route 4.20a, descending 4.20b, and thereafter following the Dales Way between Starbotton and Buckden villages: a round trip of 12.5 kilometres (7.8 miles).

4.18c From Kettlewell Wherever you seem to be in Wharfedale there are signs pointing to Kettlewell; in consequence as you finally enter the village you get a sense of having arrived somewhere. The village was once a community of important yeomen, trustees for the free-holders of Kettlewell, into whose hands the manor of Kettlewell was sold by the City of London (who got it from Charles I) in 1656. Developed from a fourteenth-century rural community, the growth of Kettlewell was undoubtedly aided by its position – even the Wharfe alters its course in deference! – its market, its fairs and its lead mines.

To reach Buckden Pike, from Kettlewell a longer undertaking than from Starbotton and Buckden, ascend first by the routes described in 4.16a and 4.16b to Tor Mere Road, and follow this until you encounter Starbotton Road. At this point ascend the hillside to the north and go left along a wall to a stile. Cross the stile and follow the wall beyond over the minor summit, Tor Mere Top, past a small tarn, and on eventually to the memorial cross and Buckden Pike summit.

DISTANCE: 7.5 kilometres (4.7 miles)
ASCENT: 490 metres (1610 feet)

By descending from the summit via Route 4.18a and returning along the Dales Way to Kettlewell, you can extend your day quite appreciably. A round trip of 18 kilometres (11.25 miles).

4.18d From Walden Strictly an offshoot of Wensleydale rather than Wharfedale, the quiet, remote dale extending

Looking down on seldom-visited Walden.

south and west from West Burton is known simply as Walden; very much a secret valley. A motorable roadway runs to Walden Head (985807), where the pastoral scene transforms into one of wild moorland. The ford beyond Walden Head is quite easy, and then begins the long, initially steep, climb to Buckden Pike, by Walden Road. This is an old packhorse route between Wharfedale and Wensleydale, and reaches the former at Starbotton.

On approaching the summit of Buckden Pike, Walden Road bends to the south to a bridlegate near the memorial cross mentioned earlier. As it does so you should, of course, simply leave it and head straight for the top of the fell. In poor visibility make a point of tending for the left of the summit (you are naturally inclined that way, anyway, by the lie of the land), then, when you meet the wall, you know you have to turn right to find the top.

DISTANCE: (From Walden Head) 3.5 kilometres (2.2 miles)

ASCENT: 385 metres (1265 feet)

Route 4.19 The Birks Fell-Horse Head ridge Contained on the north and east by Langstrothdale and Wharfedale respectively and to the south by Littondale, the Birks Fell-Horse Head ridge, just topping 600 metres (but not

On the ascent of Buckden Pike, looking across to the head of Bishopdale.

quite making 2000 feet), provides the opportunity for a long and invigorating circuit well away from the masses that sprawl across adjacent hills in the summer.

Traditionally the highest point of the ridge is regarded as Birks Fell (916764), and some maps support this claim. But a study of modern large-scale maps shows up the errors and that marginally higher ground lies further north. And this is where academic niceties fall apart as you try to apply a name to an entire ridge only to discover that a 'minor' height, Sugar Loaf in this case, is the highest point and that what has always been regarded as the principal height, isn't. Added to which the ridge curves westwards at its northern end, around Cosh, to provide yet another 600-metre summit, High Green Field Knott – for want of a better expression. It just goes to show how silly we can become if we try to impose superficial regularities on a nonconformist landscape.

The key point about this ridge is that there is no right of way along it, though the ascents are in the main bridleways. On the other hand considerate (and knowledgeable) walkers have been traversing the ridge for many years.

4.19a From Raisgill The track from Raisgill (906787) to Horse Head follows an ancient monastic way, and leaves the minor road near Hagg Beck, winding initially up steep lower slopes on a grassy track through bracken to Horse Head Gate. The trig on Horse Head is only a matter of minutes, 400 metres, north.

The prominent rounded knoll, Sugar Loaf, the true summit of the ridge, lies a little further (900 metres) in a southerly direction from Horse Head Gate. The spot height marking the summit lies on the wrong side of the ridge wall for convenience and has no distinguishing feature, though a small cairn stands not far away.

4.19b From Halton Gill Leave Halton Gill (880765) along the minor road to Foxup. Immediately after the last farm buildings take a signposted path ('To Hawes 11') through a gate, and follow this uphill as it doubles back through another gate and continues without difficulty to cross Halton Gill Beck where the path improves. Horse Head Gate lies a short way further on.

4.19c From Buckden A little distance from Buckden, along the minor road to Hubberholme, a broad track (936775), signposted 'Public Bridleway: Litton', twists above the ornamental woodland of Water Gill to a tedious upper slope relieved principally by views of Great Whernside and Buckden Pike and later, as you reach Firth Fell, of Pen y Ghent, Fountains Fell and Malham Moor. The trig on Firth Fell lies 200 metres south of the bridleway.

4.19d From Litton Though not the largest community in the dale, Litton has given its name to a valley once known as Amerdale, and Vendale in Kingsley's *The Water Babies*. This relaxing valley has everything from steep sides draped in hanging woodland and rich valley pastureland, to a wealth of flora and fauna and two charming villages with delightful pubs. Near one pub, the Queen's Arms in Litton itself, a signposted green lane ('BW Buckden') takes you to Crystal Beck followed by a steep pull up the slopes of Firth Fell to the gate in the ridge wall.

The traditional summit of Birks Fell is marked by a large cairn and lies a short way north-west of Birks Tarn, though, as with Sugar Loaf, the true summit is on the wrong side of the wall: which serves to allow me to mention that a complete traverse of the ridge, though undertaken often enough, cannot be accomplished without climbing walls. With the best will in the world this is still a sensitive indulgence, and my advice is to forget the traverse and to combine all four routes described here in one splendid double crossing of the ridge, with short extensions to Horse Head and Sugar Loaf for good measure. Use the Dales Way between Buckden and Raisgill, and the path on the south side of the River Skirfare between Halton Gill and Litton.

DISTANCE: (Round trip) 18 kilometres (11.25 miles)
ASCENT: 740 metres (2430 feet)

Route 4.20 Fountains Fell by the Pennine Way Though an easy and efficient line of ascent, the Pennine Way shuns Fountains Fell (864716) passing by its summit only a short distance to the east in an expression of indecent haste, it seems, to be among more shapely mountains to the north. Once the property of the Cistercian Order based at Fountains Abbey, near Ripon, Fountains Fell and its attendant summits, Knowe Fell and Darnbrook Fell, make pleasant walking, most notably in winter when the black, peaty ground is frozen.

Setting out for the bogs of Little Whernside.

4.20a From Silverdale Leaving the minor road from Stainforth to Halton Gill at 844715, the Pennine Way slants across the north-western slopes of Fountains Fell before tackling the steep northern face. Follow the Way as it climbs abruptly to the wall across the summit which it meets at a stile 500 metres north-east of the highest point, and close to a deep shaft once used to mine coal. The shaft is now only partly fenced and, like others in the vicinity, represents a danger, especially in misty conditions.

From the stile the Pennine Way continues ahead and down to Tennant Gill, but for the summit of Fountains Fell simply turn right, once over the stile, and follow the wall to the large cairn on top.

DISTANCE: 3.5 kilometres (2.2 miles)
ASCENT: 245 metres (805 feet)

4.20b By Tennant Gill The section of the Pennine Way that courts Tennant Gill follows a track made in the late eighteenth century for mining. It leaves the Arncliffe–Malham road at 884691 (signposted) and climbs uneventfully to the stile at the wall near the summit described above, where you simply turn left for the top.

DISTANCE: 4.3 kilometres (2.7 miles)
ASCENT: 285 metres (935 feet)

The cliffs of Malham Cove.

▲ *Malham Cove.*

The games climbers play at Malham Cove.　　　　　　　　▲

The extensions from Fountains Fell to its subsidiary summit and Knowe Fell to the south and Darnbrook Fell to the east are detailed in the circular walk described in Route 4.21.

Route 4.21 Knowe Fell, Fountains Fell and Darnbrook Fell The area around Malham with its impressive cove and tranquil tarn is understandably popular with rock climbers and tourists of the motorised variety. And it is traversed, taking in both these honey pots, by the Pennine Way, which brings its own species of humanity – the bog trotter. Inexplicably, the Pennine Way effectively ignores Fountains Fell (864716) and its acolytes, crossing the mountains below the summit of the main fell. But this is all to the good of the walker who enjoys peaceful exploration, away from crowds, because these peaty whalebacks offer an extended, circular walk, with fine panoramas, at their best on a clear winter's day.

Begin where the Pennine Way crosses the Malham–Arncliffe road (884691) and pass through a gate to start along a path (signposted 'BW Henside Road') across the adjoining field. Both the sign and the maps denote this path as a bridleway, but a number of former gateways have now been blocked and any horse using it these days would have to possess gymnastic abilities. As you enter the field bear slightly left (don't be tempted by the gap in the wall at the top of the field) and follow a vague grassy path to a gate in a new fence, followed by a wall, crossed by a stone stile. Continue with the path across the fields, crossing walls by stiles and by gaps until, at a final stile, you cross the intake wall. Here turn right and ascend on a narrow, and sometimes non-existent, path to the dilapidated wall across the minor summit, Knowe Fell; the highest point is marked by a trig column. There are splendid views along the whole of this stretch of Malham Tarn and the distant fells of Wharfedale, Great Whernside and Buckden Pike.

From Knowe Fell, follow the wall northwards across a wide expanse of peaty terrain – the worst of it avoidable by sticking close by the wall – to the southern summit of Fountains Fell (869708 – the highest point is on the eastern side of the wall, and is unmarked). In poor visibility the wall may be followed (along its eastern side, which you can only gain with some difficulty – a stile would be useful here) to an intersection with another wall, where a right turn will take you to within 10 metres of the large cairn on the summit of Fountains Fell. In clear

West Baugh Fell Tarn.

▲ *In the upper reaches of Rawthey Gill.*

The River Rawthey. ▲

weather a more direct line may be taken between the two summits, the northern cairn being prominent from as far away as Knowe Fell. En route you will pass Fountains Fell Tarn, well worth a short diversion, though the going is understandably damp.

From the top of Fountains Fell follow the wall north-eastwards until you meet the Pennine Way, which has clambered up by Tennant Gill, at a stile. There are some mine workings and an open mine shaft close by, partly fenced; interesting, but dangerous, these originate from days when coal was won from these windswept moorland hills.

Cross the wall by the stile, and continue to follow it north-eastwards until you can recross it (at a gap) to traverse round and down to the col with Darnbrook Fell. Another wall is encountered here, which may also be crossed at gaps, and followed to an intersection with a fence. Go through a nearby gate in the fence to pursue a line for the top of Darnbrook Fell, a summit trig perched in an ocean of peat.

The ridge now turns south-east, flanking Littondale, a large tributary dale of Wharfedale. Littondale is considered by many to be the most beautiful of the dales; it is noted for its rare and varied flora, trout fishing and, just above the village of Arncliffe, the impressive crag, Blue Scar. But it's all a question of taste, and I have other preferences: Dentdale, for example.

On this final leg of the walk the objective is to regain the minor road at Nab End, above Darnbrook House, but the way is confused and barred by a number of walls. Artificial as it may seem, the best way, unless you want to plunge straight down across trackless moorland to Darnbrook Beck, is simply to follow the nearby fence (cross it first) and then the wall it shortly joins (including all its bends) until, some distance hence, you are forced to turn right. Descend to pass through a gate, on your left, and follow the rough farm track which ensues, paralleling a wall, to a stile (a short way down to the right, and protected by a line of barbed wire) crossing yet another wall. Maintaining height for as long as possible, cross the ensuing fields until finally you have a clear run down to the road, joining it at 905704. The return along the road to your starting point is neither as long nor as arduous as you might expect.

DISTANCE: 14 kilometres (8.75 miles)
ASCENT: 350 metres (1150 feet)

On the banks of the River Rawthey.

▲ *Looking towards the source of the River Nidd on Great Whernside.*

Nidderdale.

Route 4.22 Yockenthwaite Moor Yockenthwaite Moor (909811) forms the long northern flank of Langstrothdale, and tumbles northwards into Bardale, Raydale and Cragdale, its waters feeding both the Ure and the Wharfe. For a long time during the preparation of this book I was kept at bay by its reputation as second only to Kinder Scout in terms of bogginess. I can imagine that in really foul conditions it is a reputation well earned, but the days I spent there came after a prolonged dry spell, and I found the going far better than expected. There are, in any case, extensive grassy stretches, and most of the bogs can be avoided with ease.

For a long and not unpleasant walk begin at Long Slack Gate (860838) at the highest point on Oughtershaw Road, which runs between Hawes and Buckden. Descend immediately into a section of rough ground and cross a fence to follow a dilapidated fenceline heading east across Fleet Moss — this, for the record, is the worst section of the whole trip, and is soon passed, making this a better approach than the alternative from Buckden. As you cross Fleet Moss the fenceline almost disappears, only an occasional post remaining to guide you on, but a wall soon

▼ *Lunch on the summit of Great Knoutberry Hill.*

The Three (Five?) Old Men of Gragareth.

The summit of Fountains Fell.

appears and steers you towards Jeffery Pot Scar, a neat escarpment coming as quite a surprise in an area renowned for bogs.

Continue with the wall running south-east until Oughtershaw Tarn comes into view. This is a remarkable setting, the tarn lying virtually on the watershed, Fountains Fell, Pen y Ghent and Ingleborough peering over the intervening Birks Fell ridge. The wall gives way to a dilapidated wall (at a stile), and nearby (before the stile is crossed) there is a neat, natural shelter for one (or two friends!) beneath some rocks.

The stretch passing the tarn is understandably boggy, and follows the wall to the foot of a short rise from which you can peer across Deepdale Gill to your distant objective, still some way off. On one visit to the tarn golden plover piped incessantly, lapwings dive-bombed me, sandpipers bobbed about everywhere, curlew, meadow pipits and skylarks filled the air with sound, while the ubiquitous grouse simply stood back and chuckled. To cap it all black-headed gulls were nesting by the tarn, under the patrolling gaze of four Canada geese.

By following the wall, which after the tarn you should have on your left, it is possible to bypass the peat hags spilling down into Deepdale. Any attempt at short-cutting this section will only lead you into difficulties; stay with the wall until, at a junction (899817 – on the left), you can cross it to ascend along another wall towards a stile. Follow the second wall, ignoring the stile, until it bends left, and from here cast yourself into the adjacent trackless summit cap of boggy groughs. These are nothing like so deep as those on Kinder, and many of them have reached bedrock, making passage much easier. Even so, it helps to have a general idea of where you want to be before you enter this final stage. The summit, a small grassy patch sticking up above the surrounding peat, is marked by a trig point.

DISTANCE: 7 kilometres (4.4 miles)
ASCENT: 130 metres (425 feet)

It is possible to continue the traverse eastwards to meet the track from Stalling Busk to the Bishopdale road, with a descent either south to Buckden or north to Semer Water, but this section of ground is most difficult, and certainly not worth considering as a line of ascent. Alternatively, the 1:25 000 map shows a number of opportunities to descend into Langstrothdale, to follow the road back (and up) to Long Slack Gate.

Route 4.23 Rogan's Seat The grouse moors of Rogan's Seat (919031) sprawl massively to the north of Swaledale,

On the summit of Dodd Fell Hill.

Nine Standards Rigg.

Outershaw Tarn on Yockenthwaite Moor.

bounded on the east by Gunnerside Gill, once an important lead-mining centre, and on the west by a sudden
northward swing of the dale as it follows the course of the
river up a series of attractive falls – the Kisdon, Catrake
and Wainwath Forces. To the north lies another summit,
commonly known as Water Crag, and beyond that the Tan
Hill Inn, the highest pub in England, and no doubt a key
objective for Pennine Wayfarers.

Given the open and desolate nature of the moors
culminating in Rogan's Seat, it is feasible, with a certain
determination, to reach the summit from virtually any
direction, but there are few rights of way, and even fewer
obvious lines of ascent.

The approach from the Tan Hill Inn has a certain
appeal, particularly towards the end of the day, but much
better, in my view, is an ascent from the south, from
Gunnerside. This has the advantage of having a broad
track all the way to the summit (one that can be followed in
mist); it affords a return via Gunnerside Gill – a place of
great interest to industrial archaeologists and anyone else
fascinated by lead mines – and the grey village of Gunnerside also has its places of alcoholic refreshment, if such be
your need.

Leave Gunnerside on the minor road to Ivelet. Footpaths, not very clear ones, take to the hillside almost
immediately as you leave the village, but there is merit in
continuing to the start of the broad track (signposted
'Private Road' – though it conveys at this stage a legitimate
right of way) at 941984. Double back on this track and
follow it easily across the upper slopes of Gunnerside Gill.
Walkers wanting to take in the minor top, Black Hill,
should leave the main track at the point of its bend to
ascend north-westwards on an indistinct footpath.

Continue, ascending gently, into Botcher Gill Nook, to
Botcher Gill Gate. The track bends here, a shooting box
close by, but continues quite clearly, eventually to descend across the hillside westward to Swinner Gill. Almost
due south of the summit a second track is met, heading

north. Here you must quit the right of way to reach the summit, making this an appropriate moment to reassert the point that these are active grouse moors, calling for every consideration from walkers. The summit itself, a broad, flat and featureless affair, is marked by a small cairn on a broad peaty uplift. Nearby, a larger cairn on a peaty topknot disputes supremacy, but fails.

DISTANCE: 7.7 kilometres (4.8 miles)
ASCENT: 440 metres (1445 feet)

The continuation to Water Crag simply takes the highest line around the gathering ground of Blakethwaite Gill, an untracked and wet proposition.

DISTANCE: 2 kilometres (1.25 miles)
ASCENT: 25 metres (80 feet)

To return to Gunnerside, head due east from the summit of Rogan's Seat, or south from the top of Water Crag, to enter Blakethwaite Gill. There is much evidence here of the lead mining which occurred in this region in the mid-nineteenth century, and the many ruins and mines are a source of endless fascination in themselves. A good track runs down the valley from the Blakethwaite mine, but it is the less obvious track, close by the gill, which needs to be taken. This continues into Gunnerside Gill itself, finally entering an area of woodland not far from the village, to which it returns by a path leading to the bridge in the village centre.

The walk up Gunnerside Gill, signposted at the bridge, is an ideal excursion on days of poor visibility, and is justly popular.

Section 5 – High Peak

	MAP REFERENCE	HEIGHT (m)	1:50 000 OS MAP
High Peak			
Kinder Scout	085875★ 084876★ 087876★	636	110

Bleaklow Head	092959	633	110
Kinder Low	079871	633	110
Crowden Head	096881	632	110
High Shelf Stones	089948	621	110
Hartshorn	115877	604	110
Grindslow Knoll	110868	601	110
Brown Knoll	084852	569	110
Lord's Seat	112835	550c	110
Margery Hill	189957	546	110
Mill Hill	061904	544	110
Back Tor	198910	538	110
Mam Tor	128836	517	110
Lose Hill (Ward's Piece)	153854	476	110
Win Hill Pike	187851	462	110

★ Three summits of equal height

Saddleworth Moor

Black Hill	078047	582	110
Featherbed Moss	046012	541	110

ROUTES
5.1   Black Hill from Crowden
5.2   The Saddleworth Edges from Binn Green
5.3   Bleaklow from Longdendale
5.4   Bleaklow and High Shelf Stones
5.5   Kinder Scout
5.6   Kinder Downfall
5.7   The Mam Tor Ridge
5.8   Margery Hill and Howden Edge
5.9   Back Tor and Derwent Edge
5.10 Win Hill Pike from Hope
5.11 Stanage Edge from Hathersage

The High Peak, also known as the Dark Peak, comprises much of the northern half of that area commonly, but incorrectly, known as the Peak District. The old name for the district is Peakland, appearing in the Anglo-Saxon Chronicle for 924 as 'Peaclond', meaning 'the land of the hill dwellers' rather than the land of the peaks. In Saxon times the district lay on the northern edge of the Kingdom of Mercia, and in a seventh-century charter the people living here were called 'Pecsaetna' – 'Pec' probably from the Old English 'peac', meaning a hill, though not necessarily a pointed one, and 'saetna' from 'Saete' or 'saetan' meaning 'dwellers'.

The southern half of the district, known generally as the Low or White Peak, is a splendid undulating plateau of Carboniferous limestone, most exquisitely seen at its best in Dovedale, the Derwent valley, especially around Mat-

▼ *Along Grinds Brook.*

Along Grinds Brook.

lock, and in the Wye valley. Predictably, given such a proliferation of limestone, the region abounds in caverns, and many of these, particularly around Castleton, have become major tourist attractions.

The High Peak, on the other hand, lies further north, within easy reach of Manchester and Sheffield, and comprises a vast expanse of wild, gritstone moorland, covered by a rich topping of heather, bilberry and tough, resilient grasses. A clear demarcation between the two regions occurs along the line taken by the great Mam Tor ridge, which separates the limestone of Hope Dale on the south from the preponderance of dark weathered sandstone on the north. But it is for its overlying blanket of peat, and its numerous deep black groughs (steep-sided water courses cut into the peat), as much as anything else, that this part of the Peak is renowned, a little unfortunately, perhaps, for the region as a whole is most beautiful. Among the walking fraternity, excursions upon Kinder Scout and Bleaklow are the source of many a tale of courage, stoicism, fun, mayhem and stupidity. Daniel Defoe, not the most reliable of travelling writers, positively hated the Peak, describing it as "the most desolate, wild and abandoned country in all England". Clearly his sensibilities were more finely attuned to the ordered lands of the south. Or perhaps his vision of it was coloured by its reputation in court circles as a place of exile for recalcitrant wives! On the other hand there is a measure of truth in his description, for Kinder and Bleaklow in particular experience weather conditions that are often grim. Grey, lingering cloud cover is a constant feature, and even in summer the incidence of fine, clear days is low. And unlike, say, the Lake District, where rainfall simply makes life a little uncomfortable for a while, in the Peak the effects of rain remain for much longer. In July 1973 over seven inches of rain fell in only a few hours, turning the peat blanket to a sodden, almost fluid morass. Since peat gives up its water only slowly, the plateaux remained impenetrable for weeks. Many walkers, myself included, find the mounds of peat encountered on Kinder and Bleaklow an especially trying obstacle; perhaps one way of coping with it is to think of it as black snow and to adjust your walking style accordingly, kicking steps, for example, instead of slithering about all over the place.

North of Bleaklow, the River Etherow flows through the valley of Longdendale to join the Goyt, and this traditionally is regarded as the northern extremity of the Peak. But, for convenience, I have extended this section of the book a little further to take in Black Hill and Featherbed Moss on the Saddleworth Moors.

The bleakness of the peaty plateaux, however, only serves to heighten the verdant loveliness around the marginal areas, Edale, Hope valley, Woodlands valley, and

▼ *The summit of Kinder Scout.*

▼ *Kinder Downfall.*

the upper reaches of the Derwent. All are remarkably beautiful, and in spite of the drowning of valleys to form reservoirs remain so, with an abundance of high- and low-level routes for the walker.

The Peak, like every region of Britain, has its record of man's development. But it was the monasteries of the Middle Ages that were the first to make any great use of the region, establishing farming settlements in the valleys and using the moorlands for grazing, becoming the first major sheepfarmers in England. Later, large private landowners came, turning their lands to support the increasingly fashionable field sports, with the introduction of the Scottish mountain hare and red grouse, both of which

▼ *Edale Cross.*

▼ *Ascending to Bleaklow from Longdendale.*

were perfectly at home among the heather and bilberry, and capable of withstanding the harsh conditions of winter.

It was this new development which, well into the present century, ensured that no trespass was tolerated on the high plateaux. And this in turn led to the mass trespass on Kinder in 1932, about which more is written in the Introduction to this book.

Suffice it to say that the Peak, whether High or Low, Dark or White, is now immensely popular, a major tourist attraction, where both walkers and rock climbers, holidaymakers and day-trippers are welcomed, and a worthy contributor to the total splendour of our mountain heritage.

All except the last of the walks contained in this section may be followed using the Ordnance Survey 1:25 000 Outdoor Leisure Map for the Peak District (Dark Peak area), and it is assumed that interested walkers will use this more detailed map (in an area where detail is often needed) in preference to the conventional 1:50 000 map. Placenames and other features are from the larger-scale map.

Route 5.1 Black Hill from Crowden The ascent of Black Hill (078047) from Crowden is something Pennine Wayfarers generally tackle on their second day heading northwards. In terms of simple beauty it is not the most well-endowed summit; Black really does mean black, especially on the summit, where the trig point stands isolated in an ocean of peat. But there is something attractive in this forbidding landscape; it is a natural environment little affected by man, where only Nature itself has any impact. Admittedly, you need to see it on a good day to appreciate the point, while anyone venturing here alone in poor conditions is asking for trouble.

Begin from the car park adjoining the A628, near Crowden Youth Hostel (074994), leaving by the rear of the car park to pass some toilets before reaching a lane. Turn left along the lane and continue until you encounter a

On the summit of Bleaklow.

Pennine Way sign pointing towards Laddow Rocks. This fine stand of rocks has long been popular with the rock-climbing fraternity, offering climbs at all grades, and is easily reached along a good path.

Just before you reach the Rocks Oakenclough Brook provides some delightful cascades. Once across the brook a path continues beneath the Rocks, providing you with the best view of them. This is a line now preferred by many on the Pennine Way, but offers less of a view than the original route above the Rocks, which gives a good retrospective of the Bleaklow massif. If you take the high road be careful not to trek left on a path leading to Chew Reservoir and Greenfield.

The weird forms of the Bleaklow Stones (this is The Anvil) are enough to go to anyone's head!

Beyond Laddow Rocks the upper and lower paths merge, and the valley opens out as you near the head of Crowden Great Brook, with a vast expanse of wild, rolling moorland before you. The going now becomes distinctly wet, and in other than perfect conditions calls for considerable navigational expertise. By way of making life a little easier one of the Peak Park's ubiquitous 'Access to Open Countryside' signs stands about one kilometre from the summit at 071041, and beyond that there is a tall cairn.

The summit also carries the name 'Soldier's Lump', a name deriving from the Corps of Royal Engineers who constructed the trig. Everywhere the scene is one of

▼ *Bleaklow Stones.*

▼ *G-rough going on Bleaklow.*

uncompromising black peat, but in the mid-nineteenth century the peat gave up the remains of a Great Ramsden theodolite used in the original triangulation in the late eighteenth century.

DISTANCE: 7.5 kilometres (4.7 miles)
ASCENT: 370 metres (1215 feet)

If returning by the same route it is advisable to take a compass bearing, even in good visibility, to ensure that you strike Meadowgrain Clough rather than one of the streams, Far Grain for example, which flows in quite the wrong direction!

Alternatively (and better if you wish to make a circuit) you may head for the long descending ridge of Tooleyshaw Moor, and across White Low and Westend Moss, or descend to pick up a good path (an old shooters' path) running with Crowden Little Brook back to the Brockholes quarry behind the Crowden Youth Hostel.

Route 5.2 The Saddleworth Edges from Binn Green It is hardly surprising that the difficulties encountered on the higher reaches of some Peakland summit plateaux has led walkers to evolve a necklace of walks around their edges, where the ubiquitous peat has drawn back sufficiently to expose the bare millstone grit beneath. These are most popular along the eastern side of the Derwent

Burning heather on the Bleaklow moors.

valley – Margery Hill, Back Tor and Stanage – and on Kinder and Bleaklow. But the Saddleworth Edges with their attendant reservoirs, fretting at the doorstep of Oldham and its suburbs, though less well known, have long been popular with local walkers.

Walkers conditioned always to reach a summit may argue that these edge walks simply snap at the heels of the problem rather than getting to grips with it. But there is an attraction in these bleak moorland fringes that often outweighs the dubious merit of battling with unremitting terrain higher up. A walk along the Saddleworth Edges ranks unquestionably among the finest, and yet motorists travelling along the A635 between Greenfield and Holmfirth may scarcely give a second glance to this apparently uninviting landscape, where dark brown caps have a sorry look about them and shrink from gritstone edges as if apologising for failing to achieve more spectacular shape or form. The walker prepared, however, to venture this way will find the recesses of Greenfield Brook and Birchen Clough, and the walk which ensues, full of interest, with buzzard, sparrowhawk, kestrel, curlew, golden plover, wheatear, skylark and meadow pipit as frequent companions.

Begin from the Binn Green picnic area (018044 – shown but not named on maps), and descend a flight of steps leading into a small copse of conifers, and to a squeeze stile

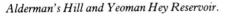

Alderman's Hill and Yeoman Hey Reservoir.

giving access to the reservoir road. Turn left here and continue to the dam to Yeoman Hey Reservoir (1880). Follow the service track around the left (western) side of the reservoir until in due course you arrive at Greenfield Reservoir (1903).

The ascent along Birchin Clough involves crossing and re-crossing the stream, which can be difficult in spate.

Along Greenfield Brook.

On the Saddleworth Edges above Dove Stones.

As you leave the reservoir behind you enter Greenfield Brook, a pleasant series of cascades in a wild and rocky setting. High above you, on the right, you can pick out a large split rock on the skyline. This is the Trinnacle, to which you will aspire in a short while.

In due course Greenfield Brook divides beneath the craggy brow of Raven Stones into Holme Clough (left) and Birchen Clough (right). Follow the path into Birchen Clough, noticing as you do the dark tunnel on your right, which sends water through a long aqueduct into Dove Stone Reservoir. Do not be tempted to explore this tunnel! Follow instead the course of Birchen Clough, crossing from side to side as necessary, but eventually entering a narrow section above a small cascade. The path, much less obvious now, presses on along the line of the brook, but you can leave it to strike up the hillside on your right to gain a conspicuous path doubling back above the line of Birchen Clough. From this coign of vantage a spectacularly expansive panorama unfolds across the tops of the Saddleworth Moors, quite unsuspected from below, with wild and rocky valleys reminiscent of remote Scottish glens. As you follow the edge path so the rock architecture improves until quite soon you are at the Trinnacle, a fine free-standing pillar of rock, split, as its name suggests, into three. Walkers with a good head for heights will experience no difficulty clambering on to the highest point, but don't feel it is obligatory. As is often the case with rock climbs, getting down is more intimidating than going up.

Your next objective along the edge is the Ashway Cross, a memorial to a Member of Parliament killed in a shooting accident. There is, however, a short detour along a narrow path not easily located shortly after leaving the Trinnacle. This leads to a large cairn known as Major's Cairn, another memorial, this time to a dog, Major, who with his owner spent a good deal of time wandering these moors. If the path is missed the simple expedient of ascending left from the edge path will bring you within sight of it within a few minutes.

From Ashway Cross the path bends to cross Dovestone Clough, before resuming its progress along the edge above another fine escarpment of gritstone faces. A short way further on you reach yet another memorial, to two climbers killed in 1972 in the Dolomites, and beyond that encounter a unique dwelling, Bramley's Cot, constructed

---

▼ *The author of The Trinnacle, Ravenstones (Photo by Tom Perry).*

One of the many memorials along the Saddleworth Edges.　　　　▼

against a face of rock in a most ingenious way. Whether it was ever completed and used is not clear. Possibly it was called a 'cot' because it was a partly completed 'cottage' . . .

Continue along the marginal path with a few unavoidable patches of peat to contend with, noting as you do the obvious gully across the valley, Wilderness Gully, scene in 1963 of reputedly England's largest avalanche in which two climbers were killed.

There is an opportunity along the edge to descend to Chew Brook if you wish to curtail the walk, but otherwise follow the path round to the dam of Chew Reservoir, built in 1912, and the highest reservoir in England.

By following the reservoir service road you can make a speedy descent to the valley bottom, where in summer shoals of would-be adventurers gather around the dam of Dovestone Reservoir and along its shores. From the dam it is only a short walk back to the Binn Green picnic area using either the broad path beside the reservoir, or ascending to a stile above the reservoir's unusual circular overflow to gain a path back to the start.

DISTANCE: 13 kilometres (8 miles)
ASCENT: 255 metres (835 feet)

Route 5.3 Bleaklow from Longdendale Longdendale is the long upper valley of the River Etherow, though you will see precious little of the Etherow now, much of its course having been drowned in a succession of large reservoirs. Constructed between 1848 and 1862, the reservoirs were built to serve Manchester and surrounding towns, and unlike other reservoirs up and down the country do little to enhance the scenery; these reservoirs are altogether far too noticeably man-made. To add insult to injury the valley, which must have been beautiful once, is further despoiled by two roads (where surely one would have done), telegraph poles, electricity pylons and a disused railway which disappears into the barred and shuttered maw of the Woodhead Tunnel.

Thankfully, you can avert your eyes from this unhappy scene and gaze instead upon a rugged and steep escarpment rising swiftly to the high plateau of Bleaklow (092959), with just enough breaks along its length to tempt the experienced walker/scrambler into an occasional diversion from recognised routes – Wildboar Clough is a prime example, but appropriate only to walkers who are also competent on rock. Other walkers may content themselves with an ascent via Torside Clough, the line taken by the Pennine Way, and a route surprisingly less tormented by the ubiquitous peat than might be expected, though it has its moments.

To facilitate a full day's walking on Bleaklow the route that follows describes a circular tour starting and finishing at Crowden. It is, however, only suitable for a clear day, and should not be attempted in poor visibility.

Begin from the car park (toilets adjacent) near the Youth Hostel in Crowden (074994), and exit from the rear of the car park (as if going to the toilets) to follow a lane northwards for a short distance until you can go left, and almost immediately pass through a gate. Follow the track beyond, passing in due course a Pennine Way signpost pointing towards Laddow Rocks. Continue ahead and eventually you will return to the A628, along which you must bring yourself to walk for 600 metres until you can descend to cross the dam of Torside Reservoir.

Once across the dam continue to what remains of a level crossing, turn right, and in a few strides ascend to a gate in a wall near a small parking place. Walkers wishing simply to ascend Bleaklow and return the same way may elect to start the walk from this parking spot (057981). The rest of the route follows the Pennine Way, and is amply identified where necessary, as it ascends the hillside behind Reaps Farm and scampers along Clough Edge. Most of the way this is a delightful approach but, as Torside Clough beneath you starts to close in, quagmire conditions return for the short stretch to Wildboar Grain, though this is the only really bad section on the ascent.

The Pennine Way turns to follow Wildboar Grain, of necessity crossing the main stream flowing into Torside Clough. Where the two streams meet a careful search will locate a tiny walled spring, constructed for the benefit of packhorses; this is John Track Well, and a source of clean spring water rather than the peaty brew which flows nearby.

Tracks ascend on both sides of Wildboar Grain, meeting up later to direct you to the summit of Bleaklow, named Bleaklow Head, a plateau of sandy gravel with the ever present peat hags lurking all around like wolves at bay.

DISTANCE: 7.5 kilometres (4.7 miles)
ASCENT: 430 metres (1410 feet)

There is little shelter on the top of Bleaklow, though some may be found in the comparative comfort of the Wain Stones a short distance away.

The next section in this circular tour makes for Bleaklow Stones, a weird and fascinating group of weathered rocks overlooking Alport Moor and the Woodlands valley. The distance between Bleaklow Head and the Stones is a mere two kilometres (1.25 miles), though it seems ten times the distance, and the going in-between is best described as g-rough! A visit after prolonged rain is not recommended.

A line of stakes makes a valiant effort to direct you across intervening ground that defies all attempts to establish a clear path. Given the right weather conditions most people would see a funny side in the passage to the Stones, but in bad weather survival is likely to be uppermost in one's mind.

Many parts of the Kinder and Bleaklow plateaux are renowned for outcrops of weather-fashioned gritstones, to which man, as is his wont, has attributed fanciful names. The Bleaklow Stones are no exception, the most readily baptised being The Anvil, though many others capture the imagination.

To return to Bleaklow Head is probably more floundering than a body can withstand in one day. Fortunately an acceptable alternative, with only a few groughs to contend with, is at hand.

Aim, from the Stones, for the upper reaches of Far Black Clough, the gradual descent of which will bring you first to a peaty path along the true right bank, and then to a broad track used to service grouse butts on the moors from which the A628 and the upper River Etherow may easily be reached in the vicinity of Woodhead Tunnel. The going along Far Black Clough is quite pleasant after the struggles of the plateau.

Woodhead Tunnel and its immediate surrounds is a sorry sight now, but it was not always so. The tunnel, cutting through the watershed of the Pennines, was constructed in 1838–45 for the Sheffield, Ashton-under-Lyne and Manchester Railway, and, at 3 miles and 66 yards, was the longest tunnel in the world when it was built. Designed mainly to take Yorkshire coal to the factories and mills of Lancashire, the tunnel was first engineered by C. B. Vignoles, who was later replaced by Joseph Locke. In 1847–52 a second tunnel was constructed, but since both tunnels only carried single tracks by the mid-twentieth century they were desperately inadequate. Between 1949–54 Balfour, Beatty and Company constructed a third tunnel for electric trains, and the completion of this coincided with the last steam train to pass through the original tunnel, after which it was adapted to take electricity power cables.

The line of the railway, gravel now and a little tedious to walk on, is the best way of returning to Crowden, better at least than walking along the roadway, and not unattractive once you pass beneath the pylons and can gaze out across Woodhead Reservoir without the intervening iron-mongery to mar the view.

DISTANCE: (Round trip) 18.4 kilometres (11.5 miles)

Route 5.4 Bleaklow and Higher Shelf Stones This route

tackles Bleaklow (092959) from the south and south-west, the former being the line pursued by the Pennine Way, and introduces the walker to much the same conditions he will face on an ascent from Longdendale. In poor visibility the terrain is dangerously void of helpful landmarks, and prolific in its confusion; it follows then that such circumstances require considerable experience and competence if a safe journey is to be completed.

5.4a From the Snake Pass The pass takes its name from the Snake Inn (114950), rather than the other way round. And the inn in turn derives its title from the serpent which is the crest of the Cavendish family who owned great tracts of land around Bleaklow until the estate was taken by the state in lieu of death duties; in 1959 it passed to the National Trust.

A stile (088929) across a fence near the top of the Snake Pass shows the way to Bleaklow, and in a short while crosses a feature known as Doctor's Gate. Much travelled now by modern walkers, Doctor's Gate lies on the line of a Roman road linking the fort of Melandra, west of Glossop, with Navio, at Brough near Castleton; it was certainly the original crossing of these high moors before construction started on the A57 in 1821 at the hands of the renowned Thomas Telford. There is some confusion about the naming of Doctor's Gate. There has been an unproven suggestion linking Doctor's Gate with Doctor Faustus and the Devil, and a view that it is a corruption of Dog Tor, though there are no tors in the form of dogs now. More likely it is named after Dr. John Talbot, who was vicar at Glossop between 1494 and 1550; certainly Camden referred to the route as Doctor's Gate in 1789. Modern historians, however, are now inclined to the view that Doctor's Gate is simply a medieval packhorse route linking two otherwise remote valleys.

Beyond Doctor's Gate the Pennine Way next encounters a feature known as Devil's Dyke, a long, straight trench cut through the peat, and possibly an ancient boundary, the precise purpose of which seems lost in antiquity though it is marked simply as a drain on maps. After Devil's Dyke the Way continues on a line intermittently marked by posts, but a diversion along another prominent dyke from Alport Low will bring you to the summit of Higher Shelf Stones.

Higher Shelf Stones is doubtlessly the best vantage point on Bleaklow, though I would prefer the view northwards from above Torside Clough were it not for the clutter of Longdendale, and it is well worth resting here a while before resuming the trek to Bleaklow Head. Nearby will be found the remains of a B-29 Super Fortress which crashed in November 1948; it is not a little ironical to hear of RAF trainee pilots having erected a memorial near the spot – they use it as a marker during training exercises!

Worthwhile as the diversion to Higher Shelf Stones undoubtedly is, you will pay for it as you press onwards; a plethora of peat groughs presents a formidable challenge only relieved by the stony confines of Dowstone Clough as you near the summit.

DISTANCE: 4 kilometres (2.5 miles)
ASCENT: 120 metres (395 feet)

If you take the diversion to Higher Shelf Stones you will miss one important feature of this route, namely a traverse of a narrow neck of land forming the watershed of England, somewhere between Hern Clough and Crooked Clough. Here in the wild vastness of Bleaklow these two streams, heading for widely different destinations, flow only a few metres apart. The precise line of this natural wonder is, however, easier to detect on a map than on the ground, and walkers in search of it may well return thoroughly underwhelmed.

5.4b From Old Glossop Modern Glossop, sometimes referred to as Howardtown after Bernard Edward Howard, 12th Duke of Norfolk, who watched over the shaping of 'New' Glossop until his death in 1842, evolved from the eighteenth- and nineteenth-century growth of the cotton-manufacturing industry, doing so in a way which left the older part of the town largely untouched, so that Old Glossop still retains much of its former character.

Take the road, Shepley Street, which leaves the minor road through Old Glossop at 042947, and follow this as a walled lane, part of Doctor's Gate mentioned above, passing to the north of limpet-shaped Shire Hill, which dominates the town. A well-used path ascends the Lightside ridge sandwiched between Yellowslacks Brook and Shittern Clough (an unfortunate naming, but meaning what it suggests). As you ascend the ridge a wall to your right gives way to a fence, which leads to the top of Yellowslacks, the scene of an attempt in the early 1960s by farmers to destroy a fine section of crags popular with rock climbers. Under the pretext of protecting their sheep from loose rock they brought in contractors to blast the rocks to the ground. Thankfully, for the climbers, two attempts failed to do the job properly, and in the end the Peak Planning Board resolved the difficulties by negotiating access agreements.

Dowstones Clough may be used from Yellowslacks to reach the top of Bleaklow, aiming for the prominent Wain Stones, from where it is a short walk to the large cairn on the summit.

DISTANCE: 5 kilometres (3.1 miles)
ASCENT: 460 metres (1510 feet)

It is equally pleasing to ascend to Bleaklow via Shelf Brook and Doctor's Gate, thereafter following the Pennine Way. This gives a longer and more circuitous route. But its use as a descent at the end of the day, following the brook as it murmurs down from the bleakness of Coldharbour Moor, is much to be preferred, and readily facilitates a round trip from Old Glossop.

Route 5.5 Kinder Scout A vast plateau covered with a profusion of moorland plants, Kinder Scout (085875) is the highest part of the magnificent gritstone country of the High Peak. It may come as a shock then to find that the principal height in this 'rocky' terrain is better renowned for a less endearing feature, a treacly, glutinous topping of thick, black peat. Everyone curses it, everyone struggles across it, and all the while grouse chuckle at you and tell you to 'go-bak, go-bak': sound advice indeed after prolonged wet weather. Yet for all its shortcomings this is a natural morass, and has a certain fascination, unlike the mess you may find in the valleys, trampled as they are by marauding visitors that flock to Edale in their thousands every year.

Part of the problem, of course, lies in the fact that Edale is the customary beginning (and only infrequently the end) of the Pennine Way, and so, given the usual dropout rate for walks of this magnitude, has to cope with far more attention from would-be Wayfarers than do other villages along the way. Nor is Edale permitted any rest in winter, when the easy slopes, particularly of Grindslow Knoll, bring skiers and tobogganists to the valley.

Of Kinder Scout just about every published comment advises against endeavouring to cross the plateau in poor visibility. One might be forgiven for thinking that so popular a route as the Pennine Way may be in some measure waymarked, but it isn't. And once beyond the confining walls of Grindsbrook Clough, facing the remarkable landscape of the plateau, the going can become unremittingly tough.

There must be some reason why the actual summit of Kinder is not crossed by the Pennine Way. Perhaps in the days when the Way was being pioneered no one was sure just where the highest point was. It is by no means certain now; a cairn with a pole sticking from it, bearing the metric height '636' and the non-metric '2088', is generally taken for the summit, but the Ordnance Survey in their meticulous wisdom have come up with two other, equal heights not far distant, and these are similarly marked. Certainly when I first visited Kinder I found the summit only with what I still insist was Divine assistance.

Having said that people frequently come and go in the mists of Kinder, maps flapping in the breeze, compasses festooned around their necks, an eager, anticipatory look in their eyes, to all intents and purposes perfectly aware of where they are, and where they are going. But it wouldn't surprise me if people have gone up there and never been seen again!

One word of advice then: if lost on Kinder head either north or south, and sooner or later you will hit a road. It may not be the one you want, but it will be infinitely safer than wandering about mystified.

5.5a By Grindsbrook Clough This is the conventional start to the Pennine Way, and leaves the village northwards, to cross Grinds Brook by a footbridge. Steps lead to an open field with the recesses of Grindsbrook Clough beckoning beyond.

Continue along the Way, a quite acceptable and interesting start to the day, pressing on into the narrowing upper reaches of the clough, until finally you reach a fork

Major's Cairn on Saddleworth Edge.

in the route, both lines of which flow with water feeding the brook you have been following thus far. Ascend left, steeply, on a short scramble to the edge of the plateau.

By heading west on a vague track you will in due course intercept a feeder of Crowden Brook. At this point the Pennine Way (described by the Ordnance Survey as 'un-defined') turns north (and later north-west), but for the summit cairn you must cross the brook and scramble up the other side, and then follow a bearing from the brook to the summit. The terrain does nothing to facilitate walking on a bearing, so when you do reach the summit don't be in too much of a hurry to leave it, it is one of only a few identifiable features on the plateau, and should be used for further directional bearings.

DISTANCE: 5.3 kilometres (3.3 miles)
ASCENT: 400 metres (1310 feet)

5.5b By Jacob's Ladder and Edale Cross This route pursues what is regarded as an alternative start to the Pennine Way, meeting up with the original line at Kinder Downfall.

Leave the village by the track heading west near the Nag's Head Hotel, and pursue the Way, signposted, if a little indistinctly, all the way to Upper Booth Farm. Some of this section is muddy underfoot (not that this should deter anyone heading for the Kinder plateau), and may be avoided by taking the minor road from Barber Booth to the farm.

Continue easily to Lee House Farm, the last inhabited farm, and on to a footbridge, formerly a packhorse bridge, at the foot of Jacob's Ladder. Beyond the ladder a wide path heads west beside a dilapidated wall until it reaches Edale Cross (407386), sheltering in its own private wind-break. The cross marks the extent of lands once owned by Basingwerk Abbey in Flintshire.

Turn north now, across a broad stile, to ascend by a wall, slightly left of Swine's Back. An earlier sign, near a gate and stile, may encourage you to pass to the east of

Swine's Back; it matters not which line you take, but the Edale Cross is a feature of interest, and the line from there better for navigation purposes. Once level with Swine's Back take a bearing for Edale Rocks; the next section of ground is especially wet, and if you are making for Kinder summit in poor visibility, you need initially to reach the trig on Kinder Low. Heading first for Edale Rocks aids your progress better than trying to stick to the Pennine Way. From Kinder Low take a bearing for the summit, and persevere with it across a seemingly endless series of groughs all against your line of approach. Always keep in mind, too, that the distance from Kinder Low to Kinder summit is a mere 800 metres. If, having travelled this distance, you miss the summit cairn, go back; to carry on could leave you wandering aimlessly about the plateau for a long time before you meet any useful navigational aid.

DISTANCE: (from Edale) 7.3 kilometres (4.6 miles)
ASCENT: 400 metres (1310 feet)

To continue to Kinder Downfall from the summit you need to head north-west into the feeders of Red Brook, itself a feeder of the River Kinder, until you intercept the alternative Pennine Way (about 400 metres), and then follow the Way north for a little over a kilometre.

Route 5.6 Kinder Downfall It is hard not to believe that the rocky amphitheatre of Kinder Downfall is the one and only redeeming feature of the High Peak's boggy moorlands; such would be an unjust belief for there is much in the High Peak to encourage and gladden walkers of all ages. But the Downfall has something of a mystique about it, as if it stands as a portent of someone's misfortune, as well as conjuring up images of jumbled boulders, rockfalls, and savage white water.

The River Kinder, above the Downfall, after all the peat groughs, comes as a pleasant surprise, having a broad bed of sand, and it is the river's plunge over the lip of the moor which causes the sensation. It is not an uncommon sight, in windy conditions, to find the water being hurled skywards as it falls over the Downfall to create a massive plume of water visible for quite some distance. Nor is it uncommon to find it bone dry!

5.6a From Edale Follow the Pennine Way as far as Crowden Brook (described to this point in Route 5.5a), and on reaching the brook turn northwards, still pursuing the Way, along the bed of the brook, first to a cairn and then beyond the gathering streams to cross the watershed into the streams that feed the Kinder. If the day is fine you may conjecture here that the streams behind you eventually feed the River Trent, and so the North Sea, while those ahead of you end up in the Mersey and the Irish Sea, for such is the case. Should mist prevail, however, your mind will be on other things!

In due course the Way passes on through the rocky passage of Kinder Gates, and so on to the Downfall, though it is not so well seen from this approach as from others.

DISTANCE: 6.5 kilometres (4 miles)
ASCENT: 395 metres (1295 feet)

5.6b Via Edale Cross From Edale or Barber Booth follow Route 5.5a as far as Edale Cross and Swine's Back, but where that route makes for Kinder Low, stay with the Pennine Way (Alternative Route), and continue to the Downfall. In many ways this is a better route, having a clear track as far as Swine's Back and a tolerably clear one thereafter along the edge to the fall.

DISTANCE: (From Edale) 8.5 kilometres (5.3 miles)
ASCENT: 390 metres (1280 feet)

The route crossing via Jacob's Ladder and by Edale Cross is an old packhorse route from the Sett valley and Hayfield to the Yorkshire markets. It is clear throughout and may be followed from Hayfield along Kinder Road (leading to Kinder Reservoir), leaving this at Bowden Bridge

(049870) for the track to Southead Farm, which in turn is left at Coldwell Clough where the route starts to climb to Edale Cross, from where the Downfall is easily reached.

This approach, especially in the lower section, does not always use rights of way, however, and so the following route is to be preferred.

5.6c From the Sett valley The quarry at Bowden Bridge featured in the mass trespass on Kinder in 1932, and is still a useful setting-off point.

Follow the minor road to Tunstead Clough Farm, once a staging post on the old packhorse route, and observe the waymarking signs around the farm buildings. Continue uphill, and then move right, through three gates in succession and on to Harry Moor. Follow the wall uphill to a stile and continue to the Three Knolls, beyond which the path continues, above Cluther Rocks (look for partially hewn millstones here), to join the Pennine Way alternative not far from the Downfall.

DISTANCE: 5 kilometres (3.1 miles)
ASCENT: 400 metres (1310 feet)

5.6d From the Snake Road The only advantage of this approach over the previous routes is one of height. Starting at the summit of the Snake Pass there is little ascent involved in reaching the Downfall. The going, however, is fairly arduous at times, and has little to commend it.

Leave the Snake Road on the signposted path and pursue the Pennine Way and the highest ground in a south-westerly direction to Mill Hill where a change of direction through ninety degrees is called for.

Continue now, still on the Pennine Way, in a south-easterly direction on to the Kinder escarpment, following the edge all the way to the Downfall.

DISTANCE: 6.2 kilometres (3.9 miles)
ASCENT: 100 metres (330 feet)

Route 5.7 The Mam Tor Ridge Forming the southern boundary of Edale (and in effect of this book), the Mam

Tor ridge, known locally as the Great Ridge, is an excellent way to begin one's introduction both to the Peak and to ridge walking generally; it is the only ridge walk of any note within the High Peak. Conveniently split in the middle, at Mam Nick, by the road into Edale, and with a car park close at hand, it is one of the most popular places in the region, providing easy walking with fine open views.

The eastern section of the ridge begins at Mam Tor (128836), one of the ancient Seven Wonders of the Peak, a distinctive hill rising at the head of the Hope valley. Given such prominence it is not surprising to find that the summit is the site of a large Iron Age fort, and well worth a visit on that account alone. Geologically minded walkers will find the ridge to be a contrasting divide between the rolling limestone uplands of the Low Peak to the south, and the higher gritstone country to the north.

The route is described here simply as a ridge walk, and like all ridge walks faces you with the problem of arranging transport between start and finish. Less energetic walkers may however gain many of the advantages of the walk by doing it in two sections from the Mam Nick car park, while more enterprising walkers can devise a valley link through Edale, enabling the ridge to be tackled using the village of Edale as a base; there are many variants to this possibility, and interested walkers might consider taking in tracks across the lower slopes of Win Hill and using Chapel Gate from Barber Booth.

Begin along the path leaving the A625 at 093825. This is an old path to Chapel-en-le-Frith, and ascends easily to a wall along the ridge. Lord's Seat is soon reached, its summit marked by a Bronze Age round barrow, suggesting that the Mam Tor site may have been occupied earlier than Iron Age times. As you approach Mam Nick the ridge narrows and shows signs of landslip, prevalent along the greater part of the way and calling for caution at all times. Follow the path leading diagonally right to a gate just below Mam Nick.

A few steps along the road bring you to a broad wooden stile giving access to a flight of steps which take you to the summit of Mam Tor. Popularity has necessitated this artificial escalator, and if your memory allows you to recall the condition of this ascent in the 1960s, and later in the 1970s, you won't begrudge a little tidy repair work. As you ascend to Mam Tor, known locally as the Shivering Mountain, keep an eye open for the ramparts of the hillfort, they are obvious enough, and spare a thought for the people who constructed them more than two thousand years ago. In places, notably on the main face of Mam Tor, landslip has removed a great slice of these ancient defences, and, for that matter, oblivious to man's puny efforts, wiped away a good chunk of the A625 between the Blue John Cavern and Castleton.

From the summit trig follow the broad path descending east of north along the line of a collapsed wall. The ridge curves and dips as it proceeds to Hollins Cross, where there is a memorial topograph. Beyond this continue to Back Tor Nook, where the collapsed north-western face provides an impressive sight, and on to Lose Hill Pike (pronounced 'loose'), the final stretch of which is relieved of the wall that has been your companion thus far. There is another topograph on Lose Hill Pike, though the view is not significantly different from earlier sections of the ridge. Looking backwards the ridge evokes a fine sense of achievement, while ahead the rocky topknot of Win Hill Pike catches the eye.

Walkers who need to return to the starting point may well find it easier to retrace their steps, and this is not an unacceptable proposition. Otherwise the way lies south-east by an obvious path leading to Townhead and Townhead Bridge, the end of the traverse.

DISTANCE: 8.5 kilometres (5.3 miles)
ASCENT: 300 metres (985 feet)

Route 5.8 Margery Hill and Howden Edge Motorised access to the upper part of Derwent Dale ends at a spot

Derwent Reservoir.

known locally as the King's Tree beneath Ronksley Moor. At certain times of the year, on Sundays and Bank Holidays between Good Friday and 31st October, you are obliged to stop at Fairholmes car park, a fairly modern affair with toilets, information point, a small snack bar, and a kiosk that does a nice trade in the hire of bicycles.

These eastern moors of the Peak reach their greatest height in Margery Hill (189957), and fall steeply to the Derwent, though never quite breaking into precipices. Instead, the hills are topped with weird and massive gritstone tors, weathered slowly, and probably too high to have been affected by the action of glaciers. East and north the hills fall to the River Don and the outskirts of Sheffield.

The headwaters of the Derwent were among the most important possessions of the monks of Welbeck Abbey in the High Peak, having derived their title towards the end of the twelfth century, during the reign of Richard I. The pattern of settlements in the valley was in the main initiated by the sheep farming activities of the monastery, principally during the thirteenth and fourteenth centuries, and remained largely intact and definable until the

Derwent Water Board drowned the topography of the valley between 1912, when the Howden Dam was built (followed by the Derwent Dam in 1916), and 1945 with the construction of the Ladybower Dam.

Beyond the King's Tree the walker moves into a wild landscape of bleak moorland, steep-sided cloughs, and constantly running water. To the east rise the Howden and Derwent Moors, remote, fascinating places, eminently suited to the walker in search of peace and quiet. The easiest means of ascent to the highest point, Margery Hill, and the Howden Edge is by the Cut Gate (originally 'Cart Gate'), an ancient packhorse route now linking the upper Derwent with the Flouch Inn, close by the River Don, on the edge of Thurlstone Moors. The line of the Cut Gate is shared with a popular long walk, the Cal-Der-Went Walk, which links Horbury Bridge, near Wakefield, on the River Calder, with Ladybower, on the Derwent.

The path along Abbey Brook in the Howden Moors.

5.8a From the King's Tree Leave the King's Tree
(168939, where there is room to park a few vehicles by the
side of the road) and pass through a gate on a broad track
leading almost immediately to a set of stepping stones
(often under water) where Linch Clough cascades into the
valley. Continue beyond the ford through conifer-clad
scenery until you can descend to a footbridge near Slippery Stones. The stones are not, as one might imagine,
another set of stepping stones, but a name derived from
the effects of a landslip many years ago.

The footbridge, a seventeenth-century packhorse
bridge, used to be sited at Derwent, downstream, but the
original site was submerged, and the bridge reconstructed
in its present place in 1959 in memory of John Derry
(1854–1937) "who inspired others by his love for the
Derbyshire and Yorkshire hills". Once across the bridge,
move left, into the mouth of Cranberry Clough, where a
signpost points the way to the Flouch Inn.

A short way into the clough it divides, with Cranberry
Clough on your right, and Bull Clough on your left. Cross
Bull Clough by a ford and ascend the path beyond climbing steeply on to the moors, with Margery Hill directly
ahead of you, and Featherbed Moss away to your right.

Featherbed Moss: Howden Moors.

The path becomes a little wet as it approaches Little Cut, but soon has you on the watershed, with only a short walk, south-east, to the summit.

DISTANCE: 3.8 kilometres (2.4 miles)
ASCENT: 275 metres (900 feet)

Continue south from the summit towards Featherbed Moss, in many ways a finer summit, but following a path along Howden Edge until you encounter a dilapidated wall. Follow the line of the wall into Howden Clough where you will find a narrow path leading through forestry down to the main reservoir track. Head north again to regain the packhorse bridge near Slippery Stones, to return to the King's Tree.

DISTANCE: (Round trip) 11.3 kilometres (7 miles)

5.8b From the Flouch Inn The Flouch Inn stands near the junction of the A628 and A616, and so is easily reached from Sheffield, Manchester, Huddersfield and Barnsley. The ascent to Margery Hill from this direction, again using Cut Gate, has long been regarded as a classic, with orthodox starting points at Penistone or Hazelhead; the Flouch Inn, however, is as good a place as any.

A short distance west along the A628 towards Longden-dale a stile gives access to a path through Crookland Wood, which you should follow to a gate below Hingcliff Common. The route ahead is well marked, and wet in places, though the moors are nothing like so harsh and savage as they seem from a greater distance, and the views become better as you ascend Mickleden Edge.

As you approach a dark ravine, Bull Clough – there is one on each side of the hill, with a watershed only a few metres wide separating the two – the character of the walk alters. The moor is here overlaid with peat, though a wide channel, Cut Gate proper, has been cleared down to firmer ground. The path wanders about trying vainly to dodge the worst of the going until finally you emerge on to Howden Edge, with the whole of the High Peak spread out before you, and the ground plunging away to Derwent beneath your feet. Margery Hill lies only a short distance south-east.

DISTANCE: 6 kilometres (3.75 miles)
ASCENT: 260 metres (855 feet)

The ascent from the Flouch Inn denies the possibility of a return to base quite as acceptable as that achieved from the Derwent valley. But walkers not wishing to retrace their steps should continue over Featherbed Moss to the head of Abbey Brook where you will find a neat path skirting the very rim of the valley. The path curves north-eastwards and then east above Hobson Moss Dike to reach the minor road along the edge of the moors on the escarpment above Agden Bridge, leaving you with a long, but not uninteresting return to the Flouch Inn. There is room to park near the viewpoint above Agden Bridge if you can persuade someone to meet you there.

Route 5.9 Back Tor and Derwent Edge The Fairholmes car park (173893), beneath the dam of Derwent Reservoir, is a well-equipped and excellent base from which to launch an assault on Derwent Edge. It has the advantage, too, that should adverse weather deter you from venturing on to the tops, a most pleasing walk around the Derwent Reservoir, or down the long arm of Ladybower as far as the viaduct carrying the A57, can be accomplished with ease and much satisfaction.

The traverse of Derwent Edge is a popular excursion, and rightly so. The main route that follows is expressed in an anticlockwise direction, being the better in my view, starting into the enticing recesses of Abbey Brook.

5.9a Via Abbey Brook Leave the car park and take the road leading towards the dam. As you complete the bend in the road (it now continues to Derwent) take a slanting path ascending, left, through the plantation to emerge beside the dam wall. When the dam is full the overspill is a remarkable sight, contrasting sharply with the serene loveliness of the reservoir itself and the conifer-clad slopes of the moorland beyond.

Continue a short distance to a step stile giving access to the broad reservoir track, which you should now follow all the way to the entrance to the side valley containing Abbey Brook. A signpost ('Bradfield' and 'Strines') points out an ascending track, leaving the main reservoir route just before Abbey Brook Bridge, that soon whisks you high on to the slopes of what is a long, smooth sided divide insinuating itself into the grassy moorland landscape of the Howden and Derwent Moors.

The Abbey Brook valley is an enchanting place, beginning innocuously as a broad-based valley, wooded in its lower reaches, but later developing a constantly twisting and turning form, enticing the walker to investigate what lies beyond the next bend. A good path travels the whole length of the valley, dodging in and out of Cogman Clough, and on past some old, scarcely discernible enclosures to Wild Moor Clough and the outcrop on the other side of the brook known as Barristers Tor. The valley continues to narrow, and is joined later by Sheepman Clough where you gain your first sighting of Back Tor and its gritstone summit.

At Sheepman Clough you have a choice. Either follow the distinct track into the clough, which later climbs to Lost Lad Hillend (not named on the 1:50 000 map), from where a good path leads to the topograph on Lost Lad, and on, rather boggily, to Back Tor. Or stay with the path along Abbey Brook, following this until finally it reaches the lip of the ravine. The path is narrow here, but quite clear, and continues across Hobson Moss to Agden Bridge. Once you reach the edge of the moor, however, strike due east across untracked ground to a small rocky outcrop beyond which a broad, wet path (not shown on the 1:50 000 map, but roughly coinciding with the boundary of the National Trust land shown on the map) leads you right, south, to Back Tor. This final section is heavy going at times, but is a small price to pay for the pleasure of clambering out of Abbey Brook rather than sneaking along the easy option of Sheepman Clough.

The summit of Back Tor is a fine array of weathered gritstone, the highest point of which is marked by a trig point. A little, easy, scrambling is called for to reach it.

DISTANCE: 9 kilometres (5.6 miles)
ASCENT: 330 metres (1080 feet)

The summit of Back Tor is one of the finest viewpoints in the Peak, and well worth the ascent for that reason alone. Someone has carved into the rocks just below the summit, "When Nature created Man, It created a Monster" – a remarkably perceptive self-indictment! And if you scout around you will discover that Mary and Jack became engaged here, on the 5th March 1933 – I wonder where they are now?

Moving south, not far from the summit, you will encounter what remains of Bradfield Gate, a solitary pillar supporting a signpost confirming to those who may have ascended by Shireowlers Wood (Route 5.9c) that they are still en route for Strines, and its thirteenth-century inn.

Carry on southwards, pursuing a broad and wet path, and passing more of the gritstone outcrops in which this area abounds, here named the Cakes of Bread, to Dovestone Tor – a miniature and less impressive version of Back Tor. A little further and, to one side of the main path, you reach the strangely shaped outcrop known as the Salt Cellar, commanding a fine position on the Edge, overlooking Derwent and the distant plateau of Kinder.

Return to the main Edge path, and continue east of south to White Tor and on to the Wheel Stones, another fine group of gritstone gargoyles said to simulate the wild flight of a coach and horses across the moor. And beyond these you will encounter a well-trodden path from Derwent to Moscar, which it is now convenient to use to return to the starting point.

Descend north-west along the path until you encounter

a dilapidated wall, beyond which the path continues to fall gently to the edge of the wooded plantations which flank the eastern side of the valley at this point. Follow the path along the edge of the plantation, and in due course you will come to a ford across Grindle Clough. A short way further pass between some ancient barns (one bears the date '1647'), and descend a slippery slope, following the line of a fence until you can cross the pasture diagonally downwards to a stile on the reservoir road. Should you contemplate reversing this route, the way is indicated by a sign reading 'Public Footpath via Derwent Edge to Moscar'.

Once on the reservoir road it is a simple and delightful stroll back to the Fairholmes car park.

DISTANCE: (Round trip) 16.5 kilometres (10.3 miles)

Walkers unfamiliar with the Peak will find this route a charming introduction, arguably as good as any you will find.

5.9b From Strines This is the shortest route to Back Tor, starting near the point where the minor road through Strines crosses Strines Dike (221909). A broad track leaves the road heading into Holling Dale Plantation, and turning west to ascend a pleasantly wooded hollow to Foulstone Delf. From here follow the path ahead to Bradfield Gate, from where the summit of Back Tor is only a short distance northwards.

DISTANCE: 2.8 kilometres (1.75 miles)
ASCENT: 260 metres (855 feet)

A return to Strines may be made by descending southwards along Derwent Edge, passing the Cakes of Bread, Dovestone Tor, the Salt Cellar, White Tor, and the Wheel Stones to reach the Moscar Path, and there heading east to Moscar, and the minor road, using that to return across Strines Moor.

5.9c Via Shireowlers Wood As with the approach from Strines, the ascent to Back Tor from the shores of the

Derwent Reservoir, via Shireowlers Wood (not named on the 1:50 000 map), is also short and sweet.

Start as for Route 5.9a, but leave the reservoir road where the stream of Walker's Clough flows under it. A path ascends steeply through the plantation to a gateway in a wall, and then zig-zags into the upper pastures until the ruins of Bamford House come into view. The path is, in the main, clear throughout, and brings you eventually to Bradfield Gate Head, from whence it is only a short walk to the summit.

DISTANCE: 4.8 kilometres (3 miles)
ASCENT: 330 metres (1080 feet)

Route 5.10 Win Hill Pike from Hope The village of Hope stands near the confluence of Peakshole Water, a comparatively minor stream coming from Castleton, and the River Noe, which descends from Edale through a gap between Lose Hill and Win Hill Pike (187851). Fancy suggests that both hills are named after two armies once opposed in battle hereabouts, though thirteenth-century documents record Win Hill as 'Wythinehull', meaning 'withy' or 'willow' hill. In support of this more prosaic rendition a few remaining willows may still be found in the plantations that cloak the northern slopes of the hill.

Looking along Stanage Edge towards High Neb.

▲ *Crow Chin: High Neb, Stanage.*

On Stanage Edge. ▲

Millstones at Stanage. ▼

'Hope' means 'an enclosed valley', which adequately describes its situation, and a well-dressing festival takes place here on the last Saturday in June, as they do at many places. Tissington and Youlgreave, for example, still observe the old customs. Hope Church, which dates from the fourteenth and fifteenth centuries, was once the centre of a very large parish extending beyond Castleton and across Edale to the rough bounds of Kinder.

For all its lack of stature Win Hill Pike loses nothing as a place of venture, and stands prominently between the Noe and Woodlands valleys. It boasts a fine gritstone-capped summit with a splendid panorama, and is well worth the attention of half a day.

The most convenient place to start is the car park in Hope village (171835). Leave by the minor road to Edale, following this for a mere 400 metres until you reach the lane leading to Killhill Bridge. Pass down this lane and under the railway to turn right on to the track leading to Twitchell Farm (178847). Ascend the steep pasture beyond the farm to a stile, from which the path continues across the ridge and down into the plantations above the Ladybower Reservoir. Once on the ridge summit, however, turn right and continue easily to the summit trig.

DISTANCE: 2.7 kilometres (1.7 miles)
ASCENT: 300 metres (985 feet)

Route 5.11 Stanage Edge from Hathersage From a mountaineering point of view the Peak has two specialities – long-distance walking, and low, but often elongated, rock faces favoured by the climbing fraternity. Stanage Edge, being the longest and most impressive of all the gritstone escarpments, undoubtedly has its place, rightfully, in the annals of rock-climbing history, having been explored since the late nineteenth century and still capable of entertaining the most modern rock gymnasts. But it is remarkable in affording lesser mortals, those who like their feet firmly on more or less level ground, a splendid and airy walk, full of interest, easy of access, and with a fine panorama.

The key to this gem is the large and attractive village of Hathersage, a gateway to the High Peak, and in whose churchyard is the reputed grave of Little John, Robin Hood's lieutenant. Many visitors to Stanage Edge, however, choose to ignore Hathersage, starting instead from car parks dotted along the minor road which runs immediately beneath the crags. If time is short, the abridged version authorised by these car parks is acceptable for a half day, just. But such brevity forces a premature introduction lacking in the fascination of seeing one's objective from afar and working steadfastly through the valley below to reach it, and denying a full appreciation of this long and rocky playground.

Begin then from the car park, near the fire station, in the village centre (232815), and on leaving the car park turn left, passing a short while later through an alleyway leading on to the main road through the village (toilets down to the left here). Cross the road and enter Baulk Lane, following this as it degenerates into a broad farm track until, at a signpost, it branches half left to pass behind Brookfield Manor. Continue along the line of a

Along Stanage Edge.

▲ *On High Neb looking to Win Hill Pike.*
  The crags of Stanage.   ▲

The summit of Stanage.   ▼

fence to a minor road, Birley Lane. Ignore the stile and footpath sign ahead, and turn right to follow the lane eastwards for a while until you can ascend left on a track leading to North Lees Hall. The hall was built by a branch of the Eyre family in the sixteenth century, and its tall, three-storeyed, castellated tower is said to have provided the setting for Charlotte Brontë's *Jane Eyre*.

Pass behind the hall and ascend a flight of stone steps to gain a track across a field, leading into a small plantation. On emerging from the plantation you find yourself immediately beneath Stanage Edge, a spectacular frieze of rock decorating the skyline, and stretching away to the right to Burbage Rocks, and to the left to Crow Chin (an identifiable beak even at this distance) and High Neb.

In spite of the temptation of the rocks above you, the first objective is High Neb. Go left, north-west, along the road until in little more than 100 metres a clear path appears ascending the open pasture beneath the rocks to a small wooded copse. Follow this, and on entering the copse pursue a better path composed of blocks of gritstone, later ascending to the rim of the escarpment. This is Jacob's Ladder (not to be confused with the one west of Edale) and is probably no more than an ancient trod that has been paved, though its structure reminds me of the Roman Steps in Cwm Bychan in the Rhinogs of Wales.

Once on the rim continue north-west with the path, almost immediately throwing away all the height you have gained to drop beneath the escarpment of High Neb. Shortly after a wall and stream descending on your right leave the main track and cross a stile on to a narrower but clear path through bracken. This leads quickly into the midst of a profusion of millstones, lying about the hillside as their makers left them, some lying flat, some half buried, others leaning, yet more stacked as if in some ancient wheel repair depot. Some possess centre holes, others are blank, the odd one or two only half finished, and here and there lie square blocks yet to be tackled; fifty, a hundred, perhaps, lie scattered, and I wonder, not so much why they were not put to use, but how the men who crafted them felt when told to abandon their work. It is a remarkable sight; and a sad one.

If your exploration of the millstone graveyard takes you to the foot of the escarpment rocks you will find a way upwards to the left of the prominent overhang. Otherwise follow the path until you can ascend to the rim by a grassy ramp. The path continues to the A57 at Moscar, and an approach is made easily from that direction.

The summit of High Neb is marked by a white trig point, and affords a splendid view across the whole of Peakland, High and Low, and eastwards to the edge of the moors looking down on Sheffield.

Along this section of the Edge you may notice a series of basins scooped out of rocks, some with curved lines like upturned cat's whiskers. All of them are numbered, and this is the clue that tells you they are man-made. They are in fact drinking bowls for grouse, sculpted at the beginning of this century by two gamekeepers who were paid one old penny a time to ensure their precious birds had a plentiful supply of water.

From High Neb follow the edge path on a long and splendid traverse to the highest point on Stanage. The scenery, especially that formed and framed by the weathered rocks of the escarpment, is consistently splendid. Near the top of Jacob's Ladder a road, the Long Causeway, a Roman road, leads north-east across Hallam Moors to Redmires Reservoirs, and affords an easy ascent to walkers based in Sheffield, though this is not so fine as the ascent from Hathersage. From the top of the escarpment you can sit and watch rock climbers at play, their expressions ranging from sheer delight to terror according to the route chosen and their skills in relation to it.

The highest point of Stanage, like High Neb, is also marked by a white trig, and is mostly easily reached from the top of the minor road between Hathersage and Ringinglow. To complete the present walk, descend to this road and follow it through Dale Bottom back to Hathersage, or, from a second minor road making ultimately for Hathersage Booths, take a path descending south-west to reach the upper part of Dale Bottom near Callow.

DISTANCE: 12 kilometres (7.5 miles)
ASCENT: 300 metres (985 feet)

Repeated faulting has, above Hathersage, added an interesting new dimension to an already fascinating corner. As well as the uniqueness of the gritstone escarpments a series of isolated, almost table-like hills rises to the south – Higger Tor, Carl Wark and Winyards Nick. These flat-topped hills, with gently sloping concave sides, rise impressively from the moorland, and a network of paths, makes them easily accessible.

Custom-built grouse drinking troughs on Stanage Edge.

Bibliography

English Mountain Summits, Nick Wright (Robert Hale, 1974)

High Peak Walks, Mark Richards (Cicerone Press, 1982)

A History of Lead Mining in the Pennines, Arthur Raistrick and Bernard Jennings (Longmans, Green and Co. Ltd., 1965)

On Foot in the Peak, Patrick Monkhouse (Alexander Maclehose & Co., 1932)

Northumbria, The Companion Guide, Edward Grierson (Collins, 1976)

The Peak District, F. R. Banks (Robert Hale, 1975)

Peakland Days, Roger Redfern (Robert Hale, 1970)

The Pennine Dales, Arthur Raistrick (Eyre Methuen, 1968)

The Pennine Playground, Walt Unsworth (Penguin Books, 1984)

Portrait of the Pennines, Roger Redfern (Robert Hale, 1969)

Walking in the Yorkshire Dales, Colin Speakman (Robert Hale, 1982)

Walking the Scottish Border, Robert Langley (Robert Hale, 1976)

Walks in North Westmorland, Sir Clement Jones (Titus Wilson, Kendal, 1955)

Walks in the Western Dales, Paul Hannon (Hillside Publications, 1987)

Walks in Wharfedale, Paul Hannon (Hillside Publications, 1985)

Walks on the Howgill Fells, A. Wainwright (Westmorland Gazette)

Wharfedale, Ella Pontefract (J. M. Dent & Sons, 1938)

Wild Pennines, W. R. Mitchell (Robert Hale, 1976)

The Yorkshire Pennines, W. Riley (Herbert Jenkins, 1934)